Dynamic Presentations

Mark Powell

COVENTRY UNIVERSITY LONDON CAMPUS
East India House,
109-117 Middlesex Street, London, E1 7JF
Tel: 020 7247 3666 | Fax: 020 7375 3048
www.coventry.ac.uk/londoncampus

 **CAMBRIDGE**
UNIVERSITY PRESS

Cambridge Business Skills

CAMBRIDGE UNIVERSITY PRESS
Cambridge, New York, Melbourne, Madrid, Cape Town,
Singapore, São Paulo, Delhi, Mexico City

Cambridge University Press
The Edinburgh Building, Cambridge CB2 8RU, UK

www.cambridge.org
Information on this title: www.cambridge.org/9780521150040

First published 2011
Reprinted 2012

Printed in the United Kingdom at the University Press, Cambridge

A catalogue record for this publication is available from the British Library

ISBN 978-0-521-15004-0 Student's Book with Audio CDs
ISBN 978-0-521-15006-4 DVD

Contents

Preparing to present

{ If there's one skill, above all others, that will help you stand out in the world of international business, it is the skill of presenting. And the further you progress in your career, the more likely it is that you will be called upon to present. In the age of technology and social networking it's easy to lose sight of this. But you'll never have more impact than when you stand up to speak in public. In professional life, competent presentations are expected. But great presentations are rare and always remembered.
Mark Powell, Mark Powell Communications

Welcome to *Dynamic Presentations*, one of a new series of courses from Cambridge University Press designed to develop excellence in business communication in English. The complete training package includes this book and CDs, an accompanying DVD with worksheets and a dedicated website containing further games and activities, feedback forms and full trainer's notes. You can access this material at http://www.cambridge.org/elt/dynamicpresentations.

The secret of successful presentations

Whether you're pitching one on one to a client, talking a small group of colleagues through the latest quarterlies or giving the keynote speech at a conference, becoming an excellent presenter comes down to three things:

- **Preparation**
- **Passion**
- **Performance**

This course will help you both prepare and perform. By the end of the course, you'll know how to start and how to finish, what to put in and what to leave out, when to stick to your plan and when to depart from it. You'll have an eye for visuals and an ear for how to use your voice. You'll have a feel for effective body language and the ability to make facts and figures unforgettable.

You'll also learn proven strategies for handling any question your audience might throw at you. And you'll try out a range of dynamic presentation techniques as you develop a style that is uniquely yours.

What about passion? Well, that's mostly up to you! After all, if you're not fired up about your talk, why should we be? But if you're thoroughly prepared and feel confident you can perform, you'll be free to connect with your audience. And all presentations, no matter how routine, need to connect. Think about it. If the figures spoke for themselves, you wouldn't need to present them! In the words of poet and biographer Maya Angelou:

If it matters to you, it will matter to them.

'People will forget what you said. People will forget what you did. But people will never forget how you made them feel.'

As you work through the ten modules in this course, you should always be thinking how you can make the skills and techniques your own. If something doesn't seem to work at first, it may be that it doesn't quite suit your style or it may just be that you need a little more practice. Be prepared to have fun and experiment. By getting your trainer to record you, you can analyse your performance using the online feedback forms (see page 94).

I hope you enjoy the *Dynamic Presentations* experience!

Presenting and you

Take a few moments before you begin the course to think about your own needs and experience as a presenter. Tick the comments that apply to you below and see how *Dynamic Presentations* can help you to improve.

☐ I can present quite well in my own language, but I'm not so sure I can translate that into English!

➡ Each module of the course contains the key words, phrases and expressions you need to present fluently in English. You'll also learn some of the special language patterns that skilful presenters use to create extra impact.

☐ I don't have much experience of giving presentations – even in my own language!

➡ The course brings together some of the world's leading presentation experts to share their insights with you. Full notes in the Key and commentary guide you towards a better understanding of how to present.

☐ I know what audiences in my own country expect, but what about expectations in other countries?

➡ In many of the modules, business people from different countries compare what different cultures are looking for in a presentation. The CDs and separate DVD contain recordings of presenters of different nationalities in action.

☐ I mostly just have to present to small groups in meetings – is that really presenting?

➡ It's all presenting, whether to an audience of one or one thousand, but you'll want to adopt a different style. Module 7 on rapport building and Module 9 on storytelling will help you to develop the right conversational tone.

☐ I sometimes have to address larger audiences at conferences – don't I need a special public speaking voice for that?

➡ No, you don't – you'll sound artificial. Your natural speaking voice will do just fine, but you'll need to use it in a slightly different way. Module 3 will show you how to add power and clarity to your delivery.

☐ I'm sure I must look so nervous standing there in front of everyone – what can I do about that?

➡ Relax. Most nerves are caused by fear of the unknown. But if you know exactly where your talk is going, there'll be no nasty surprises! Module 2 will help you here, whilst Module 6 shows you how to look calm and in control.

☐ I have so much data to refer to and my bosses expect to get a copy of my slides at the end.

➡ Give them a handout instead! And keep your slides simple and clear. Module 4 gives you tips on designing visuals and how to avoid data-dumping. Module 5 explains how to make dull figures come alive.

☐ My greatest fear is of being boring – how do I keep my audience awake?

➡ It's essential to get off to a good start, as that sets the tone for the rest of your talk. Module 1 offers you some options here. There are also dozens of incredibly simple 'tricks of the trade', which you can learn in Module 8.

☐ I'm not comfortable telling jokes (and in a foreign language!), but how else can I connect?

➡ There are many ways to connect with your audience and jokes are at the bottom of the list! Modules 7, 8 and 9 will open your eyes to a whole range of possibilities. Module 4 tells you how to get the right visual support.

☐ At least I can prepare for my talk, but when it comes to questions and answers, I'm up against the audience alone!

➡ You're not alone if you've rehearsed with a colleague. And not if you create the right atmosphere with your audience. Module 10 shows you how Q&A can actually be a highlight of your presentation.

1A Opening and closing

{ People tend to remember openers more than any other part of a presentation, except perhaps for the closing remarks.
Andrew Leigh, Maynard Leigh Associates, www.maynardleigh.co.uk

The secret is: have a good beginning, a good ending and keep them as close together as possible!
George Burns, actor and comedian }

1 What's more important in a talk: how you start or how you finish? Which do you find more challenging? Compare with a partner.

2 According to communication expert Andrew Leigh, there are four stages to opening a presentation. He calls these the A, B, C and D of openings. What do you think those letters stand for?

1 Capture your audience's interest instantly = A _ _ E _ T _ _ N
2 Explain what they will gain from the talk = B _ N _ F _T
3 Show them you have the authority to speak = C _ _ D _ B _ _ _ _ Y
4 Give them a route map of the presentation = D _ R _ _ T _ _ N

3 Now match the openings below to the stages in **2**. There are two openings for each stage.

a	b	c	d
In the 60 minutes it will take me to give this presentation, 7,000 US businesses will go bust.	In my 15 years in Silicon Valley I've learned quite a bit about managing risk.	Somebody once said: 'a brand is a promise'. But what happens when that promise is broken?	By the end of this morning's talk you'll know how to say 'No' and feel good about it.

e	f	g	h
My presentation this afternoon is in three main parts. Feel free to interrupt as we go along.	What I hope you'll get from this afternoon's session is a clearer idea of how CRM works.	I was fortunate enough to be part of the team at VW that developed the original Golf GTI.	Today we're looking at options A and B. And I'll be happy to take questions at the end.

4 What ways are there of capturing your audience's interest right at the start of a talk? With a partner complete the mind map opposite, using the phrases in the boxes.

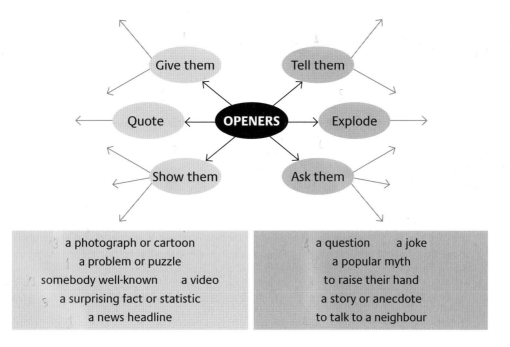

a photograph or cartoon	a question a joke
a problem or puzzle	a popular myth
somebody well-known a video	to raise their hand
a surprising fact or statistic	a story or anecdote
a news headline	to talk to a neighbour

5 🔊 1.02 Listen to the openings of five different presentations. After each extract discuss the questions below with a partner.

Extract 1: What two pieces of information does the speaker open with? Did they surprise you? In two words, what's his presentation going to be about?

Extract 2: What popular myth does the speaker explode? What two examples does she give to support her case?

Extract 3: What does the speaker ask her audience to do? She draws an analogy between backing up your hard disc and going to the dentist. What's the similarity?

Extract 4: The speaker introduces the subject of competitiveness in three ways: a quote, a joke and a task. Which works best for you?

Extract 5: How does the speaker show his audience that he really understands their business? How does he introduce his company?

6 Which openings in **5** do you find the most effective?

7 Some of the presentation openings you've just listened to are listed below. Write in the missing words.

| imagine   joke   know   like   misconception   raise   said   turn |

a Did you .... that ...?

b Could I ask you to .... your hand if you ...?

c Could you .... to a partner and discuss ...?

d Just .... what it would be like to ...

e I think it was ... who ....

f There's a common .... that ...

g My favourite .... about that is ...

h How would you .... to be able to ...?

8 Write an ABCD opening for a presentation you might give and present it to the rest of your group. If you like, use one or more of the expressions in **7** to gain your audience's attention.

1B Opening and closing

{ Try to make your last line or two truly eloquent, meaningful, touching, accurate and wise.
Always memorise your last few lines. This is the time to deliver straight to them: eye to eye,
person to person. Try to leave them with a thought that will continue to provide an echo
after you stop.

Sonya Hamlin, Sonya Hamlin Communications

1 Many of the techniques you can use to open a presentation will also work well to close
one. But this is your last chance to get your message across. How far do you agree with
what Harvard Law School presentations coach Sonya Hamlin has to say about closing a
talk?

2 🔘 1.03 Listen to the closing moments of four presentations and number the techniques in
the order you hear them.

dramatic summary ☐   famous wise words ☐   call for action ☐   heart-felt message ☐

3 In your opinion, which of the closes in **2** does best what Sonya Hamlin says it should do?

4 Group the expressions according to which closing technique they can best be used for.

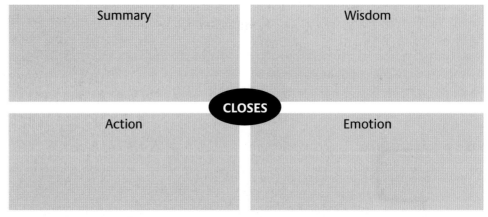

Summary	Wisdom

CLOSES

Action	Emotion

a Let's take a look back at what we've spoken about this morning.

b I'm reminded of the words of ...

c Now let's get out there and ...!

d If you take just one thing from this talk, take this ...

e In the end, this is what matters

f Here, at a glance, are the main points I've made ...

g So, how to sum up?

h I'm counting on you to ...

i We have a saying where I come from ...

j So what does all this really mean for you – personally?

k In a nutshell, then ...

l In the famous words of ...

m So, next time you ..., remember to ...

5 Communication skills trainer and bestselling author Andy Bounds has some useful advice about summarising your talk at the end. How could you avoid the danger he describes in this extract from one of his podcasts?

> When you prepare a presentation, don't use the word 'summary' at the end. The word 'summary' switches people off. Think about it. When I say the word 'summary' at the end of this podcast, you'll think 'Oh, right, he's going to repeat himself' and you'll click off and stop listening. That's what I'd do. And if you don't believe me, sit at the back of the seminar and watch what happens to the room when the speaker says 'summary'. You'll see people actually put their coats on and leave.
>
> *Andy Bounds, communications expert*

6 🎧 1.04 Read and listen to TV presenter Quentin Willson's superlative summary of the E-Type Jaguar. Think of another glamorous and brilliantly designed product you admire (a fashion item, a smartphone, a perfume, a motorbike) and use the same basic framework in bold below to sum it up to a partner.

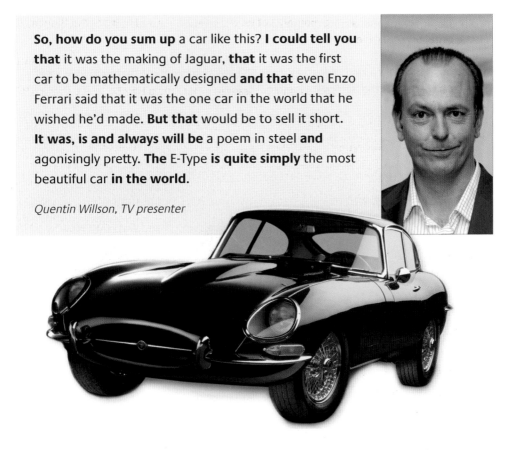

So, how do you sum up a car like this? **I could tell you that** it was the making of Jaguar, **that** it was the first car to be mathematically designed **and that** even Enzo Ferrari said that it was the one car in the world that he wished he'd made. **But that** would be to sell it short. **It was, is and always will be** a poem in steel **and** agonisingly pretty. **The** E-Type **is quite simply** the most beautiful car **in the world.**

Quentin Willson, TV presenter

7 🎧 1.05 Listen to the opening and close of a presentation about presenting. The presenter is using a technique called 'The Loop'. How does it work? Why is it so effective?

8 With a partner, prepare the opening and close for a simple product or service presentation and present them to the rest of your group. Turn to page 78 for product and service ideas or use an idea of your own. You can evaluate your performance using the feedback form on the website.

2A Smooth structure

A presentation is very much like a journey. We need to explain: 'Where are we going?' And then along that journey as we move through it, we need to explain how we're moving on. Are we making progress? And, finally, when we get to the end, we've got to close our presentation in a way that's more engaging than 'Any questions?' So finding something that reiterates those key points at the end is absolutely essential.

Rob Geraghty, The Wow Factor

1 Rob Geraghty mentions some of the ways in which a presentation is like a journey. Can you think of any others?

2 If a presentation is a kind of journey, then the ability to signpost that journey is clearly critical. Complete the 'signpost language' below:

> ask digress expand leave move return ~~start~~ summarise
> asking closing coming giving going outlining turning

I'm going to ....*start*........ off by ...

I'll be .... on to this later.

.... our main goals today.
.... you a brief overview.
.... you all a question.

Let's .... on to the subject of ...

To .... to my main point here.

OK, ... for a moment to the question of ...

Let's .... on that a little.

.... back to what I was saying earlier.

To .... for a moment.

.... the main points we've looked at.
.... you to remember one thing.
.... you with this ...

In .... , I'll just ...

3 Referring to points you made earlier in your presentation is a good way to show the coherence of your talk and strengthen your arguments. Mentioning what you'll be talking about next can build anticipation, as long as you don't get too much ahead of yourself! Decide whether the phrases below refer back or point forward and circle the appropriate arrow.

> If you don't know where you're going, you'll probably end up somewhere else.
> *Yogi Berra, baseball legend*

a Earlier we saw … ⬅➡

b This leads us on to … ⬅➡

c As you'll recall … ⬅➡

d Later we'll see … ⬅➡

e You'll remember … ⬅➡

f So, the next question is … ⬅➡

g As we discussed … ⬅➡

h This brings us on to … ⬅➡

i This goes back to … ⬅➡

j By the end of this talk … ⬅➡

4 🔘 1.06 Being able to show a logical link between your main points is very important in a presentation. Link the presentation extracts below and label the 'link phrases' with the appropriate function. Then listen and check your answers. The first one has been done for you.

cause ⟶ effect   effect ⟶ cause   action ⟶ purpose

point ⟶ contrast   point ⟶ addition   point ⟶ specification

a Turnover for Q3 is well up,

b Avoiding risk is a mistake,

c We need to constantly reassess

d A rise in the price of oil

e Demand is down 3% in Japan,

f There's no market for low quality,

and what's more, there never will be.

has resulted in reduced profitability.

whereas in the rest of Asia it's tripled.

thanks mostly to increased sales in Russia.

especially in the long term. *point ⟶ specification*

so that we don't lose our competitive lead.

g The recent flood of cheap imports

h We need to move fast

i Our share price has soared

j Now is the time to focus –

k Our website's receiving more hits,

l It's an enormous market;

as a result of the merger announcement.

and yet these have not converted into sales.

in particular on what it is we do best.

in order to take advantage of this opportunity.

plus, it's a growing one.

may lead to a price war.

5 Turn to page 79 to practise using some of the key signpost language you've studied.

2B Smooth structure

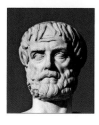

{ In making a speech, one must study the proper arrangement of the various parts.
Aristotle, Greek philosopher

1   How do you plan your own presentations? Do you have a system for 'arranging the various parts'? Compare techniques with a partner.

2   Look at the different types of presentation below and choose the one you'd be most likely to give yourself. Modify it if you need to.

a   Putting forward a proposal
b   Describing a new product or service
c   Reporting a set of financial results
d   Giving a motivational speech
e   Announcing a series of changes
f   Troubleshooting a problem
g   Announcing a breakthrough
h   Outlining a business plan
i   Pitching for (increased) resources
j   Giving a project update
k   Announcing a decision
l   Describing a new process

3   Decide which three or four of the following parts you'd want to include in the presentation you chose in 2. Then put those parts into the most effective order and explain your structure to a partner.

> action   aims   causes   competition   costs   customer need   data
> decision   future   idea   implications   investment   issue   key benefits
> main features   market potential   need   opportunity   options   past
> plan   potential objections   present   problem   procedure
> recommendations   research   results   targets   threat   us

4   🎧 1.07 Listen to extracts from three different presentations and connect up the parts as they are delivered. Each presentation begins with an attention-getter and then progresses through three stages.

Extract	Attention-getter	Stage 1	Stage 2	Stage 3
1	audience task	popular myth	opportunity	actual fact
2	proverb	threat	customer benefits	action
3	surprising statistic	product features	data	comparison

5   How did the language the presenters used in 4 help you to decide what stage of their presentation they were at?

6   Certain expressions are commonly used to talk about different parts of a presentation. Look at the sets of expressions opposite and label the part they refer to below.

> benefits ....   comparison ....   data ....   features ....
> implications ....   issues ....   options ....   popular myth ....
> potential objections ....   projections ....   pros and cons ....   truth ....

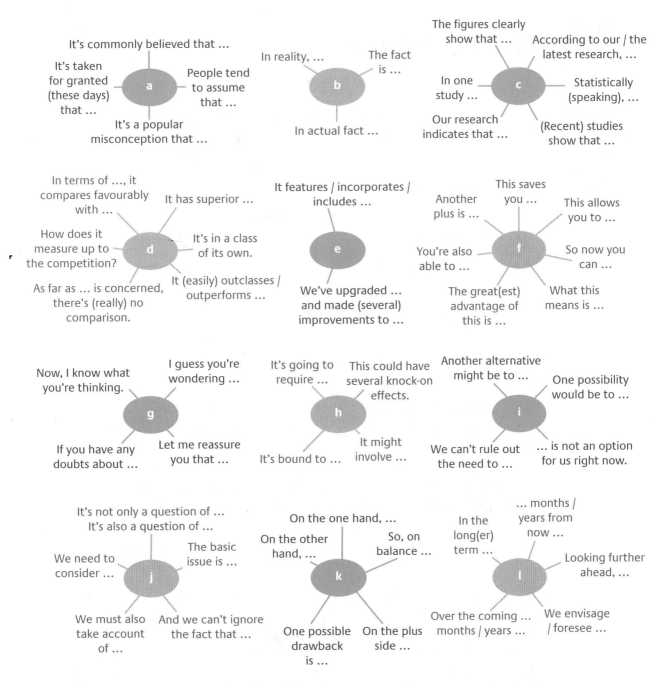

a
- It's commonly believed that …
- It's taken for granted (these days) that …
- People tend to assume that …
- It's a popular misconception that …

b
- In reality, …
- The fact is …
- In actual fact …

c
- The figures clearly show that …
- According to our / the latest research, …
- In one study …
- Statistically (speaking), …
- Our research indicates that …
- (Recent) studies show that …

d
- In terms of …, it compares favourably with …
- It has superior …
- How does it measure up to the competition?
- It's in a class of its own.
- As far as … is concerned, there's (really) no comparison.
- It (easily) outclasses / outperforms …

e
- It features / incorporates / includes …
- We've upgraded … and made (several) improvements to …

f
- This saves you …
- Another plus is …
- This allows you to …
- You're also able to …
- So now you can …
- The great(est) advantage of this is …
- What this means is …

g
- Now, I know what you're thinking.
- I guess you're wondering …
- If you have any doubts about …
- Let me reassure you that …

h
- It's going to require …
- This could have several knock-on effects.
- It might involve …
- It's bound to …

i
- Another alternative might be to …
- One possibility would be to …
- We can't rule out the need to …
- … is not an option for us right now.

j
- It's not only a question of … It's also a question of …
- The basic issue is …
- We need to consider …
- We must also take account of …
- And we can't ignore the fact that …

k
- On the one hand, …
- On the other hand, …
- So, on balance …
- One possible drawback is …
- On the plus side …

l
- … months / years from now …
- In the long(er) term …
- Looking further ahead, …
- Over the coming … months / years …
- We envisage / foresee …

7 🎧 **1.08** Listen to a manager for a financial services company giving a presentation about interdepartmental communications and complete her visual aids.

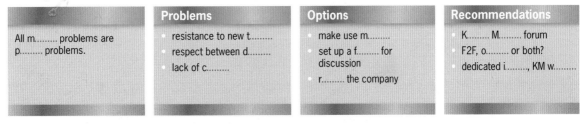

	Problems	Options	Recommendations
All m……… problems are p……… problems.	• resistance to new t……… • respect between d……… • lack of c………	• make use m……… • set up a f……… for discussion • r……… the company	• K……… M……… forum • F2F, o……… or both? • dedicated i………, KM w………

8 Turn to page 80 to practise delivering a short, structured presentation of your own, which you will present to your group. You can evaluate your performance using the feedback form on the website.

3A Voice power

> Without good delivery, the best speaker cannot be of any account at all.
> *Cicero, Roman orator*

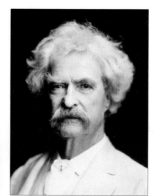

> No word was ever as effective as a rightly timed pause.
> *Mark Twain, American author*

> I learned that the spaces between words were as important as the words themselves.
> *Gerry Spence, undefeated lawyer*

1   Read the words of the three master-presenters above and work with a partner on the following questions.

   a   How far do you agree with Cicero that the most important thing in a presentation is how you sound?

   b   What's the difference between pausing and hesitating? How can a good use of pausing be helpful to both speaker and audience?

   c   Read Mark Twain's comment aloud. If you could pause just once, where would you pause? Try two, three or four pauses. Which version sounds best?

   d   Read Gerry Spence's comment aloud. Try pausing for a second after 'spaces between words'. Now try two, three and four seconds. How long is *too* long?

2   🎧 1.09 Listen to the advice of presentations coach Doug Jefferys spoken in two different ways. Which version sounds more like a conversation and which more like a presentation?

   Version 1:   Conversation ☐   Presentation ☐

   Version 2:   Conversation ☐   Presentation ☐

> In order to get your audience to really take in what you have to say, you've got to learn to stop talking – stop talking long enough for them to ingest that last thing you said, get a picture of it, try to put it into a context they know, before moving on to the next thing you're going to say. The pause is absolutely the most important thing you can do.
> *Doug Jefferys, CEO of PublicSpeakingSkills.com*

3 In which of the two versions you have just listened to does the speaker:

	Conversation	Presentation
a speak faster?		
b speak louder?		
c pause more?		
d sound more fluent?		
e sound clearer?		
f sound more interesting?		

4 1.10 Work with a partner. Listen to part of a presentation about public speaking. One of you should mark the pauses on the script below like this |. The other should <u>underline</u> the stressed words and phrases.

> 'You <u>know</u>, | there are a lot of myths about speaking in public. Myth number one is that what you actually say is only seven percent of the message. Thirty-eight percent is how you sound and fifty-five percent is how you look. But think about it. I mean, if that was true, you could go to a talk in Swahili and still understand ninety-three percent! Myth number two is that public speaking is most people's greatest fear – just above death. The comedian Jerry Seinfeld has a great joke about that. He says, "Come on, if it really was their greatest fear, at a funeral the person giving the eulogy would rather be in the box!"'

5 What type of words tend to be stressed? What do you notice about where the pauses come?

6 1.10 Listen again. When does the speaker's voice go up before a pause and when does it go down? Turn the | for each pause into ↑ or ↓.

7 Work with a partner. Take turns reading the script in **4** yourselves using the marked pauses, stresses and intonation to help you. Experiment with longer pauses and louder stresses until you find a version that feels comfortable for you. How is it different from your partner's version?

8 What is your preferred style of presenting?
- relaxed and conversational
- smooth and professional
- passionate and enthusiastic
- light-hearted and humorous

Do you adapt to suit your audience or play to your strengths?

> In the drama of organisational life, your instrument is your voice and your breath is the music.
> *Dr Louise Mahler, originator of Vocal Intelligence*

3B Voice power

> Martin Luther King did not use fillers in his impassioned 'I have a dream' speech. It wasn't the 'I have a um, you know, like a dream' speech.
> *Timothy Koegel, author of* The Exceptional Presenter

1 🎧 1.11 Listen to two versions of the same presentation. They both last about 45 seconds but how are they different?

2 Prepare a 45-second speech using one of the opening quotes on page 81 or invent one of your own. Someone else in your group will count the number of times you use a filler. Whoever *ums* and *ers* the most has to speak again!

3 In English, word stress is an important part of how we communicate, and changing what we stress can radically change what we mean. In each extract below <u>underline</u> the main stress in the two sentences.

a We haven't seen a massive improvement yet. But it's a good start.

b We haven't seen a massive improvement yet. But my guess is we soon will.

c The market may be declining. But fortunately our market share isn't.

d The market may be declining. Or this could just be a temporary blip.

e We do pretty well in the States. But we don't do so well in Europe.

f We do pretty well in the States. But not as well as we could be doing.

g Turnover is up on Q3. But profits are down.

h Turnover is up on Q3. But that was a particularly bad quarter.

i It's hard to gain a foothold in India. But not impossible.

j It's hard to gain a foothold in India. But harder still to gain one in China.

k There are a couple of points I'd like to make. And both concern cash flow.

l There are a couple of points I'd like to make. And then I'll hand you over to Jan.

4 🎧 1.12 Practise delivering the extracts in **3** and then compare with the recording.

5 Work in opposing teams. You are going to re-enact two dramatic presentations from the classic business movie *Other People's Money*.

The scene:

Andrew Jorgenson is the patriarchal chairman of New England Wire and Cable. Once highly successful, his company has not kept up with new technology and both revenues and share price are down. Lawrence Garfield, known to his enemies as 'Larry the Liquidator', a corporate financier and one of the major stockholders, is trying to persuade the other stockholders at the annual general meeting to vote him in as the new chairman, so he can carry out his plan to sell off the company's considerable assets before its share price falls any further. Of course, this will mean the closure of the firm and the loss of thousands of jobs.

Each team should choose a presenter to oppose the other team and coach them to deliver their speech by going through the text:

- marking short pauses (|), longer pauses (||) and very long pauses (|||)
- marking intonation (↑ or ↓)
- underlining stressed words and phrases
- highlighting louder and quieter parts of the speech in different colours.

Gregory Peck as Andrew Jorgenson

Danny DeVito as Lawrence Garfield

I want to share with you some of my thoughts concerning the vote that you're going to make in the company that you own. This proud company, which has survived the death of its founder, numerous recessions, one major depression, and two world wars, is in imminent danger of self-destructing – on this day, in the town of its birth. There is the instrument of our destruction. I want you to look at him in all of his glory, Larry the Liquidator, the entrepreneur of post-industrial America, playing God with other people's money. This man leaves nothing. He creates nothing, he builds nothing, he runs nothing.

This company is dead. I didn't kill it. Don't blame me. It was dead when I got here. It's too late for prayers. For even if the prayers were answered, and a miracle occurred, and the yen did this, and the dollar did that, and the infrastructure did the other thing, we would still be dead. You know why? Fiber optics. New technologies. Obsolescence. We're dead all right. We're just not broke. And you know the surest way to go broke? Keep getting an increasing share of a shrinking market. I'm not your best friend. I'm your only friend. I don't make anything? I'm making you money.

Rehearse your talk a few times. When both teams are ready, give your presentations to the annual stockholders' meeting of New England Wire and Cable. Who did the better job? Who gets your vote?

6 🔊 1.13 Listen to recordings of the speeches. How do the two speakers' styles compare? Think about pace, volume and sentence length.

7 Turn to page 82 to learn a simple method for using your laptop or PC to increase your voice power. You can evaluate your performance using the feedback form on the website.

4A Visual aids

> I hate to tell you, but, chances are, your PowerPoint slides are lousy. But don't take my word for it, let's do a little test. Show your slides to someone who doesn't speak your language. Now, you're saying 'What's he talking about? Of course, they can't read them.' Ahah! If you're expecting your audience to read your PowerPoint, you're already in big trouble. PowerPoint is a visual medium. Whether it's a chart, a graph, a picture or a cartoon, your audience should be able to understand your message just by looking at the images.
>
> *T.J. Walker, CEO of Media Training Worldwide*

1 Read the advice of leading media trainer, T.J. Walker. Then compare the two presentation slides below. Which do you think he'd prefer? Which looks more like your own slides?

2 Discuss your own preferences with a partner. Think about these features:

data load	visual impact	colour contrast
legibility	font size	scale	aesthetics

3 🔊 1.14 Listen to business people from different cultures sharing their views. Write notes on the points you agree with.

Italian
Dutch
Swedish
Japanese

4 You've been asked to give a short team presentation on family business in India. In groups, try to decide which slide opposite would be the most effective as your main visual aid.

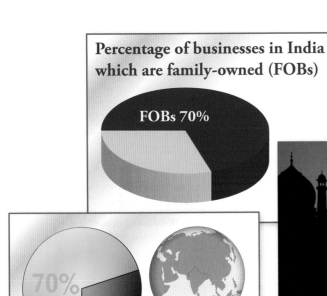

Percentage of businesses in India which are family-owned (FOBs)

FOBs 70%

70%

70% of Indian businesses are family businesses

70%

Family Business

Don't commit
career suislide!
Nancy Duarte, Duarte Design

5   Nancy Duarte is one of the world's leading presentation designers. Her company helped former US vice-president Al Gore develop his celebrated environmental talk 'An Inconvenient Truth'. What do you think she means by 'career suislide'?

6   🔵 1.15 Sometimes using real objects or 'props' in a presentation can be highly effective. Listen to business people talking about some of the best uses of props they've seen presenters make and answer the questions below.

   a   How did Apple CEO Steve Jobs demonstrate the thinness of the MacBook Air?

   b   What's the weirdest use of a prop the second speaker's ever seen?

   c   How did Cisco CEO John Chambers demonstrate the TelePresence system?

   d   What's the connection between a jeans pocket and the iPod Nano?

7   Even if your job does not involve presenting actual products, how could you use props in your own presentations? Discuss your ideas with a partner.

8   Turn to page 83 to see a selection of presentation slides before and after a designer worked on them. How far do you think they've been improved? Why?

Avoid excessive use of bullet pointing. Only bullet key points. Too many bullet points and your key messages will not stand out. In fact, the term bullet point comes from people firing guns at annoying presenters.

Don McMillan, corporate comedian

No more than six words on a slide – ever!
Seth Godin, marketing guru

1 Presenter Seth Godin's advice seems extreme. Or does it? Think of the key message of one of your own presentations – can you write it out in six words?

2 How far do the words of comedian Don McMillan remind you of any presentations you've attended?

3 The 666 Rule and 10–20–30 Rule refer to the bullet points, font sizes and number of slides you should use in your presentation. What do you think these rules might be?

4 Now look at page 65 for explanations of the 666 and 10–20–30 rules. How far do you follow these rules?

5 The slide below is ineffective. In pairs, simplify it by radically reducing the number of words and rewriting the bullet points to make them grammatically consistent. Compare your ideas with those in the Key.

A designer knows he has achieved perfection not when there's nothing left to add, but when there's nothing left to take away.
Antoine de Saint-Exupéry, aviator, author, engineer

The Five Golden Rules You Must Follow to be Effective in Presentations

- Long introductions at the beginning are a complete waste of time – get to the point!
- Never apologise for being unclear, skipping points, having difficult-to-read visuals, etc.
- It's a mistake to get too involved in the details – put those in the handouts.
- Quoting figures is not as effective as telling anecdotes and stories to illustrate your point.
- Conversation, not presentation – that's how to build rapport with your audience.

6 🔊 **1.16** Listen to part of a presentation about marketing to women and note the context in which the following key figures are mentioned.

a 85% ....
b 8/10 ....
c 75% ....
d 10% ....
e $70 m ....
f ¾ ....

7 The expressions below are all useful when presenting a slide. You heard most of them in the presentation extract in **6**. Complete them using the words in the box.

attention   axis   notice
look   talk   take   point   see

figures   question   implications
background   speak   mean
put   might   know   suggest

a Have a .... at this.
b The vertical .... represents ...
c As you can .... , ...
d Let's .... a closer look.

i To give you the .... to that, ...
j As you .... , ...
k Now, let's .... that into perspective.

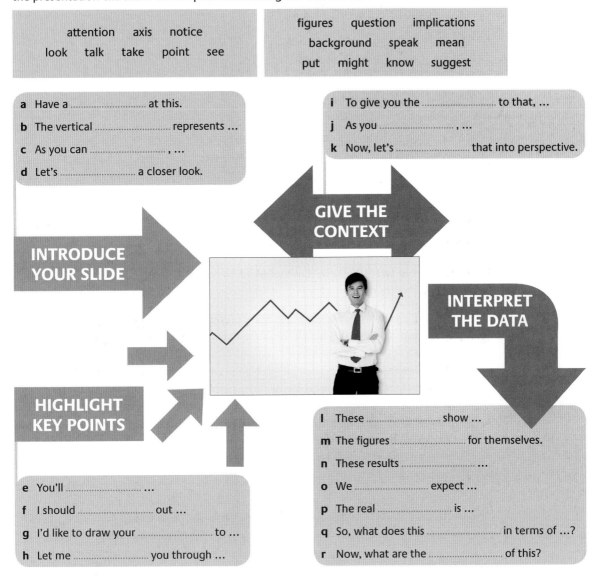

INTRODUCE YOUR SLIDE

GIVE THE CONTEXT

INTERPRET THE DATA

HIGHLIGHT KEY POINTS

e You'll ....
f I should .... out ...
g I'd like to draw your .... to ...
h Let me .... you through ...

l These .... show ...
m The figures .... for themselves.
n These results ....
o We .... expect ...
p The real .... is ...
q So, what does this .... in terms of ...?
r Now, what are the .... of this?

8 Where could you use the following adverbs in the expressions above: *clearly*, *immediately*, *presumably*, *obviously*, *particularly*, *briefly*, *frankly*, *just*?

9 In groups, choose a few of the statistics in **6** and brainstorm ideas for simple visuals.

10 Turn to page 84 to practise presenting information to your group using simple but effective visuals as support. You can evaluate your performance using the feedback form on the website.

21

5A Facts and figures

Enough data to sink a tanker. Ninety-eight percent in reserve. Know the data from memory. Make it clear that you have done a staggering amount of homework, even though you are exhibiting but a tiny fraction. Allude to the tons of research that are available. Offer one-on-one briefings if desired.

Tom Peters, management guru

1   As one of the world's most influential business thinkers, Tom Peters has given thousands of presentations. How far do you agree with him that, whenever you present, 98% of your data should be in your head, not on the screen? What are the dangers of 'data-dumping'?

2   🔘 1.17 Listen to business people from different countries and industries talking about the amount of data presenters are expected to include. Which is closest to your own situation? Compare with a partner.

3   What do you think a 'slideument' might be? Read the advice of 'Zen' presentations expert, Garr Reynolds. How could you implement his idea in your own presentations to give your audience 'the best of both worlds'?

You can't say everything in your talk. Many presenters include everything under the sun in their slides 'just in case' or to show that they are 'serious people'. It is common to create slides with lots of text and detailed charts because the slides will also serve as a leave-behind document. Big mistake. Instead, prepare a detailed document for a handout and keep the slides simple. And never distribute a printed version of your slides as a handout. Slides are slides. Documents are documents. Attempts to merge them result in what I call the 'slideument'.

Garr Reynolds, presentationzen.com

Men's extra leisure time compared with women (mins/day)

0 10 20 30 40 50 60 70

Italy
Poland
Mexico
Spain
United States
France
South Korea
Finland
Germany
Sweden
Japan
Norway

4   Look at the data in the graph, which shows the extra amount of leisure time men have as compared with women in 12 different countries. Imagine you're presenting to an audience of mostly female Polish executives. Decide what data to keep in the slide and what to leave for the handout.

Compare your ideas with other people. Who kept theirs simplest?

5 🔊 **1.18** Practise saying the following figures. Then listen to the CD.

a	14,640	**e**	$60.10	**i**	½%	**m**	⅓	**q**	1,000 cc	**u**	5.50 sqm
b	33.33	**f**	8.001%	**j**	¼%	**n**	75°	**r**	18% pa	**v**	Q3
c	1999	**g**	103 m	**k**	¾	**o**	▲ 2 pts	**s**	$1.3/€		
d	2010	**h**	6.1 bn	**l**	⅝	**p**	9:1	**t**	2,000 rpm		

6 Work in groups of four. Turn to page 85 to practise fluency with figures.

7 🔊 **1.19** Round figures are generally more memorable than exact ones. Present the information below in round figures, using the 'approximation words' in the box to help you. Then listen and compare your version with the one on the CD.

> almost   nearly   (somewhere) around   approximately   roughly   more / less than
> (just / a little / well) over / under   (round) about   (well) in excess of   just short of

   a In Q4 we saw a 19.7% increase in revenues.

   b We've managed to bring down costs by 24.9%.

   c We currently have 97 branches in 205 countries.

   d We've made a substantial investment of $499.1 m.

   e 76% of the respondents in our survey actually expressed no preference.

   f The basic model comes in 56 different versions.

   g Turnover this year was €112,687,401.

   h The project will be completed in 6–10 weeks.

> Numbers don't mean much unless they're placed in context. Recently I worked with a company that launched a 12-gigabyte memory card – 12-gigabytes! That number doesn't mean much to most people, so we put it into context. We said that's enough memory to listen to your music while traveling to the moon and back! Now, 12-gigs means something to me. Make numbers meaningful.
> *Carmine Gallo, Gallo Communications, former CNN journalist and author of*
> *The Presentation Secrets of Steve Jobs*

8 🔊 **1.20** Carmine Gallo has coached companies such as Intel, Nokia and IBM in communication skills. Read what he has to say about numbers and do what he suggests by matching the figures to the contexts (e–h). Then listen and check your answers.

   a Globally, 256 million people are involved in start-ups.

   b The world consumes 164.5 billion litres of bottled water a year.

   c The world's richest 1½% are worth around $50 trillion.

   d Apple's Fifth Avenue megastore turns over $350 million a year.

   e To give you an idea of just how much that is, it's enough to fill Loch Ness 22 times!

   f That's roughly the equivalent of selling 10,000 Mercedes-Benz cars!

   g To put that into perspective, if they joined hands, they'd circle the world 12 times!

   h That means they currently control just over half the planet's wealth!

   a .... **b** .... **c** .... **d** ....

9 🔊 **1.21** Present the original graph in **4** using round numbers and just highlighting the key figures. If you can, put it into context. Then listen to the model version on the CD.

As a presenter, nothing commands like credibility. This is especially true when it comes to presenting data. Audiences that are analytical, scientific or engineer-minded tend to look at the data with a sceptical eye – it's what they're trained to do, after all. If your data has been boiled down or clarified too much, they may feel it has been manipulated, has become 'marketing data' or is no longer substantial. To prevent these assumptions, avoid decorating your data; ornamentation can detract from credibility.

Nancy Duarte, Duarte Design

1 Nancy Duarte is one of the world's leading presentation designers. To what extent do you agree with her that there's such a thing as 'technical data' and 'marketing data'?

2 What kind of audiences do you typically have to present to?

3 Being able to accurately describe trends is an important part of presenting data. Brainstorm all the verbs you know to describe the following trends:

Which of the verbs you came up with can be converted into nouns?

4 When you want to give your audience an idea of the scale, speed and significance of the trends you're describing, you need to use modifiers. Add the modifiers in the box to the chart according to their function. Some of them may serve more than one function.

> substantial   disappointing   massive   rapid   encouraging   slight
> ~~marked~~   alarming   modest   huge   moderate   tremendous
> ~~disastrous~~   sudden   significant   fantastic   ~~sharp~~   enormous
> gradual   steady   marginal   considerable   dramatic

Scale BIG OR SMALL CHANGE?	Significance GOOD OR BAD CHANGE?	Speed FAST OR SLOW CHANGE?
++	++	++ *sharp*
+ *marked*	+	+
–	–	–
– –	– – *disastrous*	– –

5 With a partner, write descriptions of this simple bar chart using the expressions in the box.

Example: *D is marginally higher than E.*

marginally higher than   (just) as high as
by far the highest   almost as high as
not quite as   nowhere near as high as
more or less the same
considerably higher than   equally high

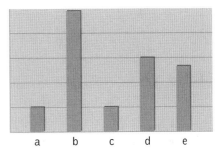

6 Put the following phrases in order from a large decrease to a huge increase:

  a more than doubled   b almost halved   c nearly tripled   d increased tenfold

  e quadrupled   f fell by a third   g increased three and a half times

7 Complete the key words below for describing markets and market share.

An inc.................... share of a shr.................... market.

A dec.................... share of an exp.................... market.

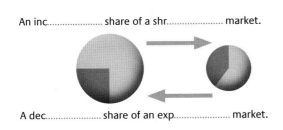

THE MARKET

be fo.............. out of

en..............

ex..............

br.............. into

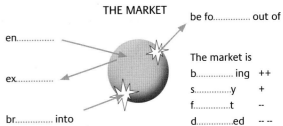

The market is
b.............. ing ++
s..............y +
f..............t --
d..............ed -- --

8 🔊 1.22 Write the missing prepositions in the presentation extracts below. Then listen and check.

The ad had an immediate impact. In January our CT rate went up .... 2½% .... just ½% .... 3% – an amazing six-fold increase!

Then in February we saw a drop .... 1¾ .... just 1¼%. But that's still well .... average.

In March the figure fluctuated .... a high .... 2 and a low .... 1%.

Finally, in April it hovered .... 1½% to finish up .... a little .... that by the end of the campaign. All in all, an excellent response!

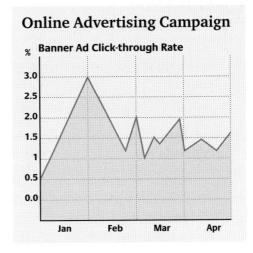

Online Advertising Campaign

Banner Ad Click-through Rate

9 Turn to page 85 to practise presenting different kinds of numerical and graphic information. You can evaluate your performance using the feedback form on the website.

6A Body language

‘Act natural’ is always good advice. But, remember, when you present, you're not speaking face to face, but face to faces. To reach out to your audience you need to be just a little bit larger than life. You are your most important visual aid.

Begoña Arsuaga, partner, Communicadia

When your body language is out of alignment with your verbal message, people believe what they see – not what you say.

Carol Kinsey Goman, Kinsey Consulting Services

1 Think about the comments of the communication experts above and discuss the following questions with a partner:

  a How easy is it to 'act natural' in front of an audience? How could you make your body language 'just a little bit larger than life'?

  b How far do you agree that your main visual aid is you?

  c When you present, in what ways do your actions 'speak louder than words'?

2 **1.23** Listen to four business people from different cultures talking about body language in presentations and answer the questions.

  a What does the Brazilian say about the age of the audience? Is it the same in your country?

  b What point does the Australian make about words and body language? Is it good advice?

  c What is the Finn's intercultural recipe for success? Do you agree with his point about content?

  d What does the Kuwaiti say about private and public speaking? Would you take his advice?

3 When presenting, the body language of the sexes tends to be a little different. Which do you associate with men and which with women?

a Move around the room more	M / W	b Hold eye contact four times longer	M / W	c Gesture towards themselves	M / W	d Gesture away from themselves	M / W
e Point and wave their arms more	M / W	f Smile and nod while listening	M / W	g Tilt the head and frown while listening	M / W	h Keep bodies fairly rigid	M / W

I speak two languages – body and English.

Mae West, Hollywood legend

4   How typical are you of your gender? How could you be a bit more gender-neutral?

5   Look at the statements below and match them to the gestures that would best reinforce
    them. Are all these gestures acceptable in your culture?

1	2	3	4	5	6
I think there are three main issues here.	I ask you, what are we supposed to do?	I wonder what the answer is here.	OK, let's take these points one at a time.	This really isn't good enough!	Let's just remember one thing.

a   b   c   d   e   f

6   Work with a partner. Memorise the short presentation extracts below, one at a time, and
    then take turns to present them. What gestures feel natural for you?

    a   As you know, the project has been a huge success.

    b   On the one hand, it's very high quality. But on the other hand, it's expensive.

    c   I think we can eliminate Option B straight away.

    d   But this isn't about me. It's about you, every one of you here today.

    e   So, what's the long-term trend? Frankly, who knows?

    f   It just isn't working. And there are two main reasons for this.

    g   We're aiming to expand our product range by 25%.

    h   So, our goal is to increase productivity whilst cutting back on costs.

    i   For us at the moment R&D is a top priority.

    j   The whole thing has been a disaster from start to finish.

    k   Profits have gone up from six to eight million dollars.

    l   Firstly, it's highly effective. Secondly, it's highly efficient. And thirdly, it's high time we
        did it.

    m   And it's powered by the tiniest microchip you've ever seen.

7   How do you rate your partner's body language overall? How does it compare with yours?

    A little bit static   Confident and expressive   A bit too theatrical

6B Body language

It has been well established by researchers that those who can effectively read and interpret non-verbal communication, and manage how others perceive them, will enjoy greater success in life than individuals who lack this skill.

Joe Navarro, former FBI Special agent and author of What Every BODY is Saying *and* Louder Than Words.

1 Do you think it's possible to show the following qualities through your body language?

> leadership   charisma   honesty   enthusiasm   confidence   conviction

2 Research has shown that people can send and receive up to 10,000 non-verbal clues in less than a minute. What postures and gestures might signal the qualities in **1**? How would you know the speaker lacked these qualities?

3 Divide the following behaviours into those which convey a sense of authority and those which create rapport. It's not just about body language, but the body plays a crucial part.

> wait   maintain lots of eye contact   use subtle gestures   talk slowly
> look slightly above the audience   ask lots of questions   stand still   use humour
> listen   imagine you're talking to a small group of friends
> imagine your presence fills the room   say less   talk low   get excited

Authority	Rapport

4 Which is more important to you when you speak in public – authority or rapport? Is it possible to have both?

5 Work in groups. Just for fun, deliver one of the following using appropriate body language – speak the words with your lips, but silently. Can your group guess what you are saying?

   a Our technological lead gives us an enormous advantage.

   b What we're experiencing is a period of steady decline.

   c In a sense, these are two opposing ideas.

   d By merging our two firms we'll enjoy significant economies of scale.

   e You can see that the new model has a much simpler, sleeker design.

   f I'd like to talk you through the different stages of the process.

6 Work with a partner. Look at the examples of presenter body language opposite. In what ways could they be distracting or create the wrong impression? Are you guilty of any of them?

7 🔊 1.24 Now listen to four short extracts from a presentation about body language and discuss these questions with a partner.

   a Why are hands so important? What makes a particular gesture distracting?

   b Why isn't folding your arms the answer to the 'hands problem'? How is it similar to standing behind a podium? What's the solution to 'the podium trap'?

   c What makes a 'hands problem' even worse? How can you guard against this?

   d What are the signs of being too energetic and too relaxed? What should you do?

8 Give a short, simple presentation to your partner – perhaps on where you'd like to be in ten years' time. Make some of the annoying gestures above as you speak and see how many they can spot!

9 Pictures a–e illustrate more examples of unhelpful body language in a presenter. Can you work out what they are?

10 Choose a subject you feel strongly about and prepare a short presentation on it. Spend 10 minutes making some notes. The template on page 87 may help. Try to make your main points as graphic and dramatic as possible. When you're ready, present your opinion and let your body follow your words. You can evaluate your performance using the feedback form on the website.

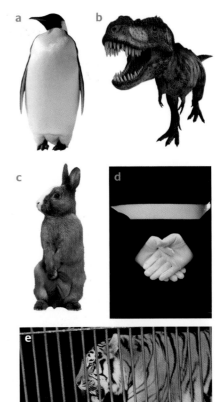

Rapport building

You rehearsed your speech thoroughly and mastered that all-important body language. But when you delivered the talk, you sensed little enthusiasm in your audience. What's going on? You're probably coming across as artificial. To demonstrate your authenticity, imagine meeting four aims: being open to your audience, connecting with your audience, listening to your audience and being passionate about your topic. When you rehearse this way, you'll genuinely experience these feelings when delivering your speech. And your listeners will know you're the real thing.

Dr Nick Morgan, Public Words

1 Dr Nick Morgan is an author, *Harvard Business Review* journalist and expert on developing authenticity and charisma as a speaker. With a partner, try to decide:

a in what ways you can show openness to your audience

b what you can say or do to connect with your audience

c how you can deeply and actively listen to your audience

d how you can demonstrate passion for your subject.

2 2.02 One simple way of connecting with an audience is to reduce the number of references to 'I' and 'you' and replace them with 'we'. Increase rapport in the statements below by changing *some* of the pronouns to the first person plural. Then listen and check your answers.

a Now, I know this is something that affects each and every one of you.

b I think you'd all agree that in the long term this is in your best interests.

c You need to be asking yourselves: what are you trying to achieve?

d So do you or don't you take up the challenge? The choice is yours.

e I've got three amazing new products I want to share with you today. So let me get started!

3 2.03 Another way to be more interactive is to use question tags. Add tags to the presentation extracts below. The first one has been done for you as an example. Then listen and check your answers.

a This isn't really so surprising, *is it?*

b But we won't let this stop us.

c We certainly can't complain.

d We've been here before.

e I said it was good news.

f You know what's going to happen.

When you are giving the same presentation many times, it is important not to let yourself get bored. Interacting with your audience is the best way to achieve this.

Mike Grabiner, former CEO of Energis

4 **2.04** Rephrasing controversial statements as negative questions makes them much more persuasive. Rephrase the following in this way. The first one has been done for you as an example. Then listen and check your answers.

a We should be focusing our attention on our core business. *Shouldn't we ... ?*

b Offshoring – this is something we need to be looking at.

c It's time we started to take internet advertising seriously.

d We've had enough of being number two in this industry.

e There's a need for more accountability at board level.

f We're in danger of losing some of our best customers.

5 **2.05** To build real rapport, your presentation needs to sound conversational. One thing you can do to achieve this is to repeatedly involve your audience. That's what the speaker below is doing. She is addressing an international group of CEOs and senior executives. Match up the seven stages of her speech in a–g with her involvement expressions in h–n. The first one has been done for you as an example. Then listen and check.

a Let's just talk about email for a moment. <u>If you're anything like me</u>, you probably wish email had never been invented!

h You'd think I was crazy, right? I mean, there are currently 1.7 billion email users out there! But let me ask you a question.

b And it's not just spam, is it? When was the last time you received dozens of emails that didn't even directly concern you?

i And would it surprise you to learn that students now hardly use email at all – except to contact professors and parents!

c So, what if I was to say to you that email, as we know it, is dead; that email will soon be as obsolete as the fax machine?

j But, you see, that's where you'd be wrong. The fastest-growing group of social networkers is actually women over 35.

d How many of you pay regular visits to sites like Facebook, MySpace or Twitter? How about texting? Most of you. Interesting.

k Raise your hand if that's happened to you. Right. I think that's something we can all relate to. Email is inescapable.

e But let me share some statistics with you. Did you know that 300 million users spend 8 billion minutes a day just on Facebook?

l And you don't need me to tell you that, together, China, India and women over 35 exercise a tremendous amount of influence!

f Now, I know what you're thinking. You're thinking, well, OK, sure, we know kids are the biggest users of Web 2.0 technology and texting.

m I mean, I don't know about you, but on a typical day I probably waste more time on email than just about anything else.

g And the biggest markets for SMS are China and India. The Chinese alone send half a trillion text messages a year!

n If, like me, you find yourself more and more involved in social networking these days, then you should already know that email is on its way out.

a *m*   b ....   c ....   d ....   e ....   f ....   g ....

6 Underline the involvement expressions the speaker uses in **5**. There are at least 16. The first one has been done for you.

7 Now prepare a short presentation with a controversial theme and use some of the rapport techniques you've studied in this module to make your speech more persuasive. There's a 'controversial ideas bank' on page 87. You can evaluate your performance using the feedback form on the website.

7B Rapport building

{
You know a little humor would make your communications more engaging, persuasive, and memorable. The good news is, you can be funnier – and you don't even have to tell jokes! It's one thing to be funny. It's another thing to spread fun. You don't have to be Oscar Wilde. You don't have to be Robin Williams. You just have to be a fun person that creates opportunities for laughter to emerge.

Doni Tamblyn, HumorRules.com

1   Doni Tamblyn is a comedian, corporate trainer and expert on using humour when you communicate. Read her comments and discuss these questions with a partner:

   a Do you agree that being fun is more important than being funny?

   b In what ways could *you* create 'opportunities for laughter to emerge'?

2   Form two groups. One group should brainstorm the advantages of using humour in a presentation, the other the possible disadvantages. Then briefly team-present your pros and cons. Which team made the stronger case?

3   💿 2.06 How could you create humour out of the following in a presentation? Briefly discuss each situation with a partner. Then listen to the story of how a presenter actually handled it and decide which of their strategies might work for you.

   a You know your audience is dying to see the new product you've just been describing.

   b You invite your audience to share their thoughts with a neighbour, but a lot of them are either sitting alone or seem uncertain how to begin.

   c There's a sudden power cut and you lose all your audio-visuals!

   d You're scheduled to give a pre-dinner talk on Valentine's Day.

   e You are the last speaker on the programme and, before you even start, your audience looks exhausted and ready to go home!

4 Humour is not the only thing that is a matter of personal taste. We know that different people also process information in different ways. Theories vary, but some of the most common intelligence types are represented in the diagram below. To key directly into each intelligence you need to vary your language. With a partner, write the letter of each presentation extract beneath the type or types of intelligence you think it's specifically addressing.

a Picture this …	**h** The basic principle is fairly easy to grasp.
b How does this sound?	**i** So, logically, …
c Let's take a moment to reflect on that.	**j** Take a minute to talk to a partner.
d Statistically speaking, …	**k** Now, you're probably saying to yourself …
e Do you see what I mean?	**l** Unfortunately there isn't time to go into depth here.
f It strikes me that …	**m** I want to share with you …
g Ask yourself …	

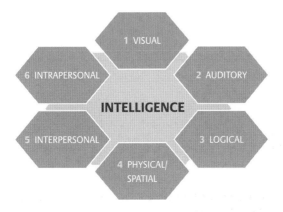

n But let's look at this another way.	**t** Does that make sense to you?
o What I'd like to do is give you a feel for …	**u** On balance, …
p I think the figures speak for themselves.	**v** To illustrate what I'm saying …
q Personally, …	**w** So far we've barely touched on the question of …
r I hear you say …	**x** Just to give you an overview of …
s Between you and me, …	**y** Let me fill you in on the background to that.

5 🎧 **2.07** Listen to some short presentation extracts. From what the presenter is doing or asking the audience to do, what intelligences do you think they're addressing?

Extract 1: ....

Extract 2: ....

Extract 3: ....

Extract 4: ....

Extract 5: ....

Extract 6: ....

Extract 7: ....

Extract 8: ....

6 Turn to page 88 to practise rapport building. You can evaluate your performance using the feedback form on the website.

Impact techniques

I want to talk a minute about repetition …
I want to talk a minute about repetition. It's very, very important
in any speech that you do two things – repetition, restatement.
You have to remember that you wrote the speech, you researched
the speech, you studied and practised the speech, you basically
married the speech. You know it, but we don't. So you have to
repeat and restate the important points. I repeat, you have to
repeat and restate the important points.
Tracy Goodwin, communication professor

1   How many examples of repetition and restatement can you find in Tracy Goodwin's
    comments? Think about words, phrases, sentences, sounds.

2   ⊙ 2.08 Create greater impact in the presentation extracts below by replacing one word
    in each with a word that has already been used. The first one has been done for you as an
    example. Then listen and check your answers.

      question
    a It's not a question of qualifications. It's a ~~matter~~ of talent.

    b I always say total quality begins with absolute commitment.

    c What's the use of setting goals if your objectives are unrealistic?

    d One thing we don't need is more data. We're drowning in information as it is!

    e A decline in the market doesn't have to mean a drop in sales as well.

    f We're still running at zero profit. But, from nothing the only way is up.

3   ⊙ 2.09 Look at the statements below and <u>underline</u> words you could repeat after a short
    pause to increase your impact. The first one has been done for you as an example. Then
    listen and check your answers.

    a First of all, I'm pleased to report that profits are <u>up</u> by 38%.
       First of all, I'm pleased to report that profits are up … up by 38%.

    b It's a cliché, I know, but this firm has always put its people first.

    c Ladies and gentlemen, it's time to face the facts.

    d So, that's what happened – what I want to know is: why did we let it happen?

    e What's really important for us to do right now is this …

    f One thing I know: we must never again lose our sense of focus.

    g Nobody likes failure, but some people are more afraid of success.

    h We've come a long way to get to where we are today.

    i And today we're announcing our biggest breakthrough ever.

4   ⊙ 2.10 A very effective repetition technique
    is to echo the first word of your statement at
    the end. This is sometimes called the James
    Bond technique. Complete the statements
    opposite by putting the same word in both
    gaps. Then listen and check your answers.

'Bond,
James Bond.'
*Sean Connery
in* Dr No

nothing	everything	anything	no one	everyone	nowhere

a .... have we been more successful than in South America – ....

b .... has ever been able to beat us on price – ....

c .... in the beta test was positive about the product – ....

d .... is beyond us if we work together as a team – ....

e .... would be better than the system we've got at the moment – ....

f .... in this market is about to change – ....

5　A mantra is a key phrase that is repeated several times throughout a speech – for example, Barack Obama's 'Yes, we can!' Think of a presentation of your own. Can you reduce your key message to a mantra of no more than seven words? Compare with others in your group. Briefly give the background to your presentation and suggest improvements to each other's mantras if you can.

'Yes, we can!'
Barack Obama

6　Repeating certain sounds can add power to your key points. Advertisers use this technique a lot. Look at the following famous examples and identify the sounds being repeated. Some repeat more than one.

Pleasing people the world over. *(Holiday Inn)*	Fly the friendly skies. *(United Airlines)*
You can be sure of Shell. *(Royal Dutch Shell)*	Don't dream it. Drive it. *(Jaguar)*
Where do you want to go today? *(Microsoft)*	Sense and simplicity. *(Philips)*
Probably the best beer in the world. *(Carlsberg)*	Functional. Fashionable. Formidable. *(Fila)*

7　● 2.11　Now replace the word in **bold** in each of the statements below with a close synonym that echoes the highlighted sounds in the rest of the sentence. The first one has been done for you as an example. Then listen and check your answers.

promoted

a　Properly priced, packaged and ~~advertised~~, this product cannot fail.

b　China is not our main market, but it may be a **significant** market in the future.

c　Of course, this is a serious problem to which there's no **easy** solution.

d　In the world of international finance this **company** remains a formidable force.

e　I know that if we work together as a **group** we can take on the competition.

f　If we cannot challenge change, then we have no **option** but to embrace it.

g　If we don't manage to break even on this by Q4 we may even go **under**.

8　● 2.12　Turn to page 88 to practise using repetition for dramatic impact. When you've rewritten and delivered your short presentation, you can evaluate your performance using the feedback form on the website. Then listen and compare your version with the one on the CD.

Is there anything you can do to get your message across with greater impact? Are there any techniques that all successful speakers use to inspire, persuade and enthuse their audiences? And, if so, can anyone learn to use them? The good news is that the answer to all these questions is an emphatic yes. The same rhetorical techniques that were originally defined by the ancient Greeks are still very much alive and well today. They are the way effective speakers speak.

Max Atkinson, Henley Business School

1 Max Atkinson is the world's top researcher into audience reactions to public speakers. In his comments above find examples of:

   a repetition of words and sounds   **b** rhetorical questions   **c** groups of three

2 Why do you think rhetorical questions are so powerful in a presentation?

3 Phrasing a key point as a question and echoing the question in the answer is often more effective than just making your point. Look at the example and transform the other statements in a similar way.

   a Piracy is the main challenge we face.
   So, what's the main challenge we face? The main challenge is piracy.

   b Viral marketing is the answer.

   c Converting leads into sales is the problem.

   d China is where the best opportunities are.

   e Big-budget advertising simply doesn't work, that's my point.

   f Give our project teams more autonomy, that's the plan.

4 **2.13** Work with a partner. Can you think of another rhetorical question you could add on to the end of each extract in **3**? Then listen and compare your ideas with those on the CD.

5 **2.14** Certain rhetorical questions are very common in presentations. Complete the ones below using the pairs of words in the box. Then listen and check your answers.

> where + go   ~~how + do~~   what + do   why + selling   what + talking
> how soon + expect   where + did   what + waiting   how much + wasted

   a We've tripled revenues in two years. So, ...*how*........ did we ....*do*......... it?

   b The whole of central Asia is one big golden opportunity. So, ... are we .... for?

   c We poured millions into this venture and it flopped. So, ... we go wrong?

d When the patents run out on this product, our competitors will legally be able to clone it. So, ... are we going to .... about it?

e We spend fifty million dollars a year on internet advertising alone. But .... of that is .... ?

f It's by far the most cost-effective system on the market. So, ... isn't it .... ?

g In spite of offering excellent salaries and benefits, we're still failing to retain key personnel. So, ... do we .... from here?

h Retooling the plants is not going to be cheap. So, ... sort of figure are we .... about?

i We've considerably stepped up our R&D activity. So, ... can we .... to see results?

6 Choose a rhetorical question from **5** or formulate one of your own and use it to create a 20-second presentation of your own product or service or one you know well. Use the following three-part structure:

Present the situation → Ask a rhetorical question → Answer the rhetorical question

7 Grouping points in threes seems to almost magically make them more memorable. Match up the three presentation extracts below:

a What will it take to achieve our goals?

b How do we plan to become a more socially responsible firm?

c Where do our key markets lie?

d In Canada, Russia and Scandinavia.

e Time, effort and tenacity.

f Through our total commitment to clean energy, sustainability and fair trade.

a .... **b** .... **c** ....

> A billion hours ago, human life appeared on earth. A billion minutes ago, Christianity emerged. A billion seconds ago, the Beatles changed music for ever ... A billion Coca-Colas ago, was yesterday morning.
>
> *Roberto Goizueta, former CEO Coca-Cola*

8 🎧 2.15 Now, to each of the extracts in **7** add a fourth point as the 'punchline'. Try delivering all four points, remembering to pause after the third. Then listen and compare your version with the one on the CD.

a But, most of all, through our commitment to people.

b But, first and foremost, Germany.

c But, above all, talent.

9 🎧 2.16 Work with a partner. Look at the notes on page 89 and rewrite them as a presentation using as many impact techniques as you can. Compare your version with others in the class. You can evaluate your performance using the feedback form on the website. Then listen and compare it with the one on the CD.

8C Impact techniques

{ Wise men talk because they have something to say; fools because
they have to say something.
Plato, Greek philosopher

1 🔊 2.17 Simple contrasts and opposites can be very effective in a presentation: good and
bad, past and present, us and them. Complete the statements below using the idea of
contrast to help you. Then listen and check your answers.

a This year we're number two in the market. This t................... n................... year, we'll
be n................... o................... .

b As they say, it's not a matter of doing things right. It's a m................... of
d................... the r................... th................... .

c I'm not asking you to say yes today. I'm a................... y................... not to
s................... n................... .

d I'm not saying it's a good option. I'm s................... it's o................... on...................
o................... .

e They say you should look before you leap. I s................... le................... ,
th................... l................... .

f Five years ago we had an idea. To................... it has be................... a
rea................... .

g If we don't seize this opportunity, so................... el................... w................... .

h We may never be the biggest, but we c................... st................... be the
be................... .

2 Choose two or three of the sets of opposites below and create a contrast for each that is
relevant to a company, product or service you know. Stand up and present them to the
rest of your group.

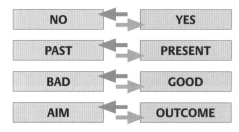

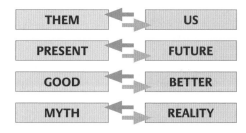

Amazing!

Incredible!

Unbelievable!

Revolutionary!

Huge!

*Steve Jobs,
Apple Inc.*

3 Great speakers make sure they create
a sense of excitement by using vivid,
expressive language – power language. The
presentation extracts opposite sound pretty
dull. Inject some enthusiasm into them by
replacing the adjectives and verbs in **bold**
with more vivid ones. Compare ideas with a
partner.

a It's a **big** market.		**e** It's an **attractive** design.	
b We've **changed** the industry.		**f** We've **reduced** costs.	
c It's a **new** product.		**g** These are **good** results.	
d We've **beaten** the competition.		**h** Revenues have **increased**.	

4 **2.18** Read the following statements. Decide where you could create extra emphasis and add the intensifiers in the order they are listed. Deliver each statement, stressing the words you added. Then listen and check your answers.

a We've done *exceptionally* well this year – *even* better than last year, in fact. (exceptionally, even)

b If we believe in this company, we need to be committed to its success. (truly, one hundred percent)

c It's done better than we expected in a short space of time. (dramatically, such)

d It's encouraging to see people working together as a team. (just so, really)

e We now dominate the sector, even though it's competitive. (totally, so highly)

f We've invested in R&D and I'm delighted to say that that investment has paid off. (heavily, absolutely, a hundredfold)

g Every unit has performed well and I believe this is the beginning of an exciting period for this company. (superlatively, genuinely, just, tremendously)

5 Metaphor is when you describe one thing in terms of another to create impact. For example, when people talk about markets being flooded or prices slashed, they are speaking metaphorically. If metaphors are used too often they lose power and become clichés. But used sparingly they can be very effective. Number the metaphors below according to the category they belong to:

> wipe out the competition   outpace our competitors
> grow our business   join forces   fall behind
> build a firm foundation for future business
> start to see the fruits of our efforts   come under attack
> win back market share   rethink our strategy   be overtaken
> play as a team   reinforce our position
> catch up with the market leaders   build a reputation
> level the playing field   get to the root of the problem
> bring out the big guns   cultivate relationships
> reconstruct our image   hit the ground running
> get in on the ground floor   be in a different league

1 Business is a sport

2 Business is a race

3 Business is war

4 Business is a construction site

5 Business is nature

6 Turn to page 89 to practise adding imagery and power to your speech.

8D Impact techniques

{ It continually fascinates me that top business managers and other professionals go on courses at considerable expense in order to learn basic oral skills – the same skills that are taught to a first-year drama student. Classical rhetoric, like good acting technique, had values we can resurrect and explore. Think of it as a series of tools that help you feel your way towards a fuller expression of words.
Patsy Rodenburg, acting coach

1 What are the most important similarities and differences between acting and presenting?

2 Whenever you combine rhetorical techniques, you multiply their impact. Use the knowledge of impact techniques you've built up to analyse the following movie extracts and find good examples of:

a rhetorical questions   c repetition of sounds   e groups of three (plus one)

b repetition of words   d contrasts and opposites   f combinations of the above

Dan Futterman in Shooting Fish

Mr Greenway, do you know why you're here? You're here to see technology at its most advanced. You're here to buy a seventh-generation computer. A computer you can talk to. A computer that'll talk to you. This is Johnson. It's the first computer to be truly free of a keyboard. Mr Greenway, nobody likes to type. Everybody likes to talk. Do you like to talk? I like to talk. Johnson here doesn't just understand 3,000 words, not just 6,000 words – the common everyday vocabulary of you or me – Johnson understands 80,024 words.

Michael Douglas in Wall Street

I am not a destroyer of companies. I am a liberator of them. The point is, ladies and gentlemen, that greed, for lack of a better word, is good. Greed is right. Greed works. Greed clarifies, cuts through and captures the essence of the evolutionary spirit. Greed in all of its forms. Greed for life, for money, for love, knowledge, has marked the upward surge of mankind, and greed, you mark my words, will not only save Teldar Paper, but that other malfunctioning corporation called the USA.

Aaron Eckhart in Thank You for Smoking

In 1910 the US was producing 10 billion cigarettes a year. By 1930 we were up to 123 billion. What happened in between? Three things: a world war, dieting, and movies. 1927: talking pictures are born. Suddenly, directors need to give their actors something to do while they're talking. Cary Grant, Carole Lombard are lighting up; Bette Davis: a chimney. And Bogart: remember the first picture with him and Lauren Bacall? She says: 'Anyone got a match?' And Bogey throws the matches at her and she catches them – greatest romance of the century. How'd it start? Lighting a cigarette. These days when someone smokes in the movies, they're either a psychopath or a European. The message Hollywood needs to send out is: smoking is cool. Most of the actors smoke already. If they start doing it on screen, we can put the sex back into cigarettes.

3 Choose one of the movie extracts in **2** and reduce it to notes you can write on five prompt cards. Try not to have more than six words on each card.

4 Deliver the presentation from your notes. Don't even try to reproduce the original! Just have fun with it and use as many impact techniques as you can. But stick to your natural style – relaxed, dynamic or whatever suits you best.

5 🎧 2.19 Listen to recordings of the three presentations. Concentrate on the way the speeches are delivered. If you'd like to, have another go yourself.

6 🎧 2.20 Impact techniques are not only useful in formal platform speeches, they can also be very powerful in more relaxed, conversational presentations. Compare the two performances below of Carly Fiorina, former CEO of Hewlett-Packard. Listen and read. Then answer the questions below.

Good morning. What you just saw is an ad that will begin running this morning. We call this ad Anthem. It's part of a campaign that will feature the stories of our customers and how they use our technology. And all of these customers that we will feature have one thing in common. Every one of them was told that what they hoped to accomplish was impossible. FedEx was told they'd never make an overnight delivery service work. Amazon was told they'd never make online retailing work. BMW's Formula One team was told they'd never make a car that rivals Ferrari. In every single case, they proved the skeptics wrong. And in every single case, HP was there. Why is this the face we have chosen to show the world? Because it's about everything we can achieve, working together. It's an affirmation of our belief that progress is not made by the cynics and the doubters, it is made by those who believe that everything is possible. Now is not the easiest time for the IT industry, or around the world, for that matter. But in these uncertain times, it is our capacity to look ahead, our capacity to build a better future, our capacity to develop practical solutions that make our work all the more essential.

Presentation at Comdex Computer Expo

a Fiorina uses one impact technique more than all the others combined. Which one is it and what effect does it have?

b What are the functions of the two rhetorical questions Fiorina uses?

c What can you say about the way Fiorina varies the length of her sentences?

d What rhetorical differences do you notice between the two speeches?

So what do I know about change? First thing I know is that everybody is afraid of something. Everybody is afraid of something. All of you are afraid of something. All of us are afraid of something. What distinguishes people who are successful in their life from those who are not is: what do you do with your fear? Some people are held back by their fears and some people choose to move ahead in spite of fear. Courage is not the absence of fear. Courage is acting in spite of fear. But because everybody is afraid, what most of the time people are afraid of is something new. The essence of entrepreneurship is risk-taking. The essence of business is risk-taking. Taking a risk is all about trying something new.

Presentation at Stanford University

7 Turn to page 90 to practise using impact techniques yourself. You can evaluate your performance using the feedback form on the website.

9A Storytelling

{ Storytelling is the single most powerful
tool in a leader's toolkit.
*Dr Howard Gardner, Harvard Professor
of Cognition and Education*

The choice for leaders in business and
organizations is not whether to be involved in
storytelling – they can hardly do otherwise – but
rather whether to use storytelling unwittingly
and clumsily or intelligently and skilfully.
Steve Denning, author of The Leader's
Guide to Storytelling *and* The Secret
Language of Leadership }

1 Consider the comments by the storytelling experts above and discuss these questions with
a partner:

  a How far do you agree with Dr Howard Gardner about the power of storytelling? What kind
  of stories do leaders need to tell?

  b Is it only leaders who need to tell stories? What about frontline managers, accountants,
  technicians and IT support staff? What about you?

  c What do you think Steve Denning means by a story told 'intelligently and skilfully'?

2 Telling stories is a powerful technique at any stage in a presentation, but particularly
at the beginning and end. Ed Brodow is an actor, author and leading negotiation skills
trainer. Read the opening opposite of his keynote speech at the Pentagon and match the
storytelling techniques he uses to the highlighted parts of the text:

  a Create drama   d Deliver the punchline   g Set the scene
  b Signal the end of the story e Involve the audience
  c Establish credibility   f Link to the theme of the presentation

A couple of years ago, a man walks into a sandwich shop in Delray Beach, Florida and orders a meatball sandwich. So the owner starts to fix the meatball sandwich when all of a sudden the customer pulls out a gun and he says: 'This is a stick-up! Give me all the cash in the register!' Now, I don't know what you would do in a situation like that. Admiral, what would you do in that situation? You'd give him the money. I sure would give him the money. What would you do? You'd give him the money. Well, that's not what happened. By the way, this is a true story. That's not what happened. The owner of the shop puts down the meatball sandwich, looks at the robber and he says: 'Listen, pal. We've had a really bad month.' He says: 'Business has been terrible. Would you settle for ten dollars and the meatball sandwich?' Now, I'm not making this up. This was in the paper. He says: 'Will you settle for ten dollars and the meatball sandwich?' So the gunman says: 'Are you crazy?' He says: 'I've got a gun here! I'm not settling for ten dollars and the meatball sandwich.' He says: 'I'm not settling for anything less than twenty dollars and the meatball sandwich!' So, the owner says: 'You got a deal!' Gives him the twenty bucks, gives him the meatball sandwich. You know what it said in the paper? It said: 'And the robber left satisfied.' … My subject today is the courage to negotiate.

3 Look back at the presentation extract in **2** and answer the questions.

   a Which grammatical tense is used more to tell the story: the past simple or the present simple? Why?

   b There are a lot of questions in the story – real, reported and rhetorical. What effect does this have?

   c Brodow quotes what the people in the story actually said. Why is this so effective?

   d How many examples of repetition of key words can you find in the story? Why is repetition so important in a story?

Ed Brodow, negotiation expert, keynote speaker and author of Negotiation Boot Camp

4 2.21 Work with a partner. Listen to Brodow's presentation. Remembering what you've learned about voice and delivery, one of you should mark the pauses and the louder parts of the extract. The other should mark the strongly stressed words (see Module 3).

5 Now combine your notes to team-present the story with energy!

6 2.22 Listen to four business people from different countries giving tips on telling stories in presentations and take brief notes under the headings below:

Rapport	Timing	Humour	Credibility	Influence

7 Work with a partner to practise retelling a story. One of you should turn to page 90 and the other to page 91.

9B Storytelling

{ People don't want more information. They are up to their eyeballs in information. More facts will not help them. A story will. A story will help them figure out what all these facts mean. If you let the 'facts speak for themselves', you risk an interpretation that does not fit your intentions. When you give a story first and then add facts, you stand a better chance of influencing others to share your interpretation.

Annette Simmons, founder of Group Process Consulting and author of The Story Factor

1 Why do you think Annette Simmons recommends telling a story first and then presenting your facts rather than doing it the other way round?

2 An anecdote is a true story about your own life. How can this be even more effective than a story about someone else?

3 **2.23** Listen to three presenters telling anecdotes and answer the questions:

a The first presenter is talking to a group of young entrepreneurs in Singapore. How does her story help her to build rapport with her audience?

b The second presenter is an Argentinian Customer Relationship Management (CRM) specialist addressing an international group of hotel managers. How does he use statistics and humour to make his point?

c The third presenter is a German business school professor talking at an international HR directors' conference. What makes his story so effective?

4 What key skills does a storyteller need? With a partner complete the mind map below using the words in the box.

| draw | quote | use | let | stick | involve | exaggerate |

_____ interesting comparisons

_____ to present tenses for greater impact

_____ gestures to illustrate the story

_____ the audience as you speak

STORYTELLING

_____ your descriptions a little

_____ actual conversations

_____ your voice reflect the emotions in the story

5 **2.24** Change the reported speech in the story extracts opposite into direct speech. And, instead of using the attitude words in bold, let your voice communicate the same emotion. The first one has been done for you as an example. Listen and compare your versions with the ones on the CD.

a She looked up from her desk and **rather angrily asked me** what I wanted.
She looked up from her desk and said: 'What do you want?'

b He **cheerfully admitted** that, to be honest, he didn't know the first thing about computers.

c He **abruptly told me** not to interrupt him when he was speaking.

d I **laughingly replied** that he'd got to be joking!

e She took me to one side and **whispered rather secretively** that she had some information I might be interested in.

f He **pointed out rather officiously** that he was afraid that wasn't his job.

g She **remarked sarcastically** that, of course, I was the world's expert on customer relations, wasn't I?

h **He yelled at the top of his voice** that he couldn't hear himself think!

6 ⊙ 2.25 Rewrite the story extract on page 90 using present tenses where they will create more impact and changing reported speech into more immediate direct speech. Then stand up and deliver your revised version, making sure you use your voice and gestures to bring the story to life for your group. Listen and compare your version with the one on the CD.

7 A certain amount of exaggeration is permissible in a good story. But this means you may need to use a wider range of vocabulary. Work with a partner. For each of the neutral adjectives below, think of a more exaggerated adjective using the initial letters to help you. Can you think of any others?

a tired (ex…)	**f** cold (fr…)	**k** beautiful (gor…)	**p** frightening (te…)
b hungry (sta…)	**g** hot (bo…)	**l** ugly (hid…)	**q** funny (hil…)
c big (en…)	**h** clever (br…)	**m** clean (spo…)	**r** interesting (fa…)
d small (ti…)	**i** good (su…)	**n** dirty (fi…)	**s** surprising (as…)
e difficult (im…)	**j** bad (lou…)	**o** strange (bi…)	**t** exciting (thr…)

8 When is the last time something surprising / exciting / interesting / strange / frightening happened to you? Briefly tell the story.

9 A 'simile' is when you say something is *like* something else. Work with a partner. Match the similes on the right to the statements on the left:

a Their IT centre was so modern.

b We got such a warm welcome in Singapore.

c It was so dark in the auditorium.

d They were so difficult to understand.

e It was so cold on the plane.

f Everyone was so happy about the results.

g It was like a family reunion!

h It was like being in the freezer at a meat-packing plant!

i It was like we'd won the World Cup!

j It was like meeting aliens from another planet!

k It was like the flight deck on the Starship Enterprise!

l It was like midnight at the bottom of a coal mine!

a …….. **b** …….. **c** …….. **d** …….. **e** …….. **f** ……..

10 You're going to build your own anecdote step by step. Turn to page 91 and follow the instructions. You can evaluate your performance using the feedback form on the website.

10A Q&A sessions

You've told a compelling story, you've designed dazzling PowerPoint slides, you've delivered your message confidently, and now you open the floor to questions. Unless you manage this part of your presentation effectively, all of your other efforts will go up in smoke. You must stand tall in the line of fire and learn how to handle tough questions.

Jerry Weissman, Power Presentation Ltd

1   Leading corporate presentations coach Jerry Weissman has worked with high-profile companies such as Cisco, Microsoft and Yahoo! How important is Q&A in the talks *you* have to give? How do you 'manage this part of your presentation'?

2   🎧 **2.26** Listen to pairs of speakers briefly comparing how they handle questions from the audience. After hearing each pair, <u>underline</u> the speaker you agree with more and explain why to a partner.

a   First / second speaker because …

b   First / second speaker because …

c   First / second speaker because …

d   First / second speaker because …

e   First / second speaker because …

f   First / second speaker because …

g   First / second speaker because …

h   First / second speaker because …

3   The speakers in **2** refer to different types of question. Complete the main question types:

a   a g........d question

b   a d....ff....c....lt question

c   an ....ff-t...p....c question

d   an unn....c....ss....ry question

e   a m....lt....pl.... question

f   a h....st....l.... question

4   Look at Kees Garman's D8 system for handling questions. What strategy or combination of strategies would work best for each type of question in **3**?

Deal with the question straight away
Define exactly what the question is first
Defuse any negativity before answering
Divide up the question into sub-questions
Deflect the question onto someone else
Defer answering the question until later
Disarm the questioner by admitting you don't know
Decline to answer the question but give a reason

Kees Garman, communications coach

5 Now, bearing in mind the D8 system, match up each of the six question types in **3** with how you might actually respond, using the sentences below.

Question type

good .... difficult .... off-topic ....
unnecessary .... multiple .... hostile ....

a I think that raises a slightly different issue.

b What are *your* thoughts on the matter?

c I think there are several questions there.

d Well, as I might have mentioned, ...

e I'm glad you asked me that.

f I'm afraid I'm not able to discuss that, but ...

g I'm afraid I don't know off the top of my head.

h OK, let's take those one at a time.

i Let me just check I understand you correctly.

j Hmm, I wonder what other people think?

k Sorry, I don't quite see the connection.

l I don't have that information to hand.

m OK, so I think your main question there is ...

n I'll find out. Can I get back to you on that?

o Ah, perhaps I didn't make that clear.

p Alicia here might be a better person to answer that. Alicia?

q Ah, yes, thank you for reminding me.

r To be quite honest with you, I really don't know.

6 2.27 You heard one of the speakers in **2** talk about the importance of repeating the questions you're asked before answering. Repeat the questions below using the words in *italics* to help you. Then listen and check your answers.

  a Are you planning to go public with this? *You're asking me whether ...*
  b Are we in a position to take on more work? *You want to know if ...*
  c How do you see the market developing? *You ask me ...*
  d What are our chances of success? *You're wondering ...*
  e When is the launch date going to be? *You'd like ...*

7 2.28 You also heard one of the speakers say that hostile questions need to be rephrased. Rephrase the questions below using the words in brackets to help you. Listen and check.

  a Why did we spend so much on this? (asking – why – scale – investment – necessary)
  b Are these figures accurate? (like me – go through – some – figures again)
  c Why is this project six months behind schedule? (have – some concerns – timeframe)
  d Is this really going to be worth it? (like – look again – some advantages – new system)
  e Is anybody actually in charge of this unit? (have – question – management structure)
  f Do you honestly expect us to support this? (not fully convinced – benefits – initiative)

8 Turn to page 92 to practise handling neutral and hostile questions.

9 Turn to page 92 to practise dealing with all the different types of question. You can evaluate your performance using the feedback form on the website.

10B Q&A sessions

After you've prepared your material, write down the twenty questions that the audience is most likely to ask. Be prepared to answer them. This may surprise you, but you will have figured out at least ninety percent of the questions.
Sue Gaulke, Successworks

I don't do much by way of thinking of all the questions they might ask and preparing answers. I do spend a lot of time thinking about the key themes, how they link together and the best way of explaining them.
Marjorie Scardino, CEO Pearson PLC

1 Think of a presentation you have given or may have to give in the future. Take Marjorie Scardino's advice and list the key themes of your talk – list no more than three. Work out how you could link them together.

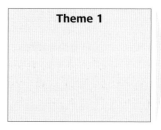
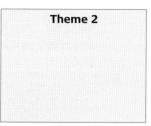
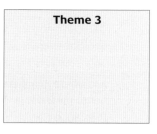

Theme 1	Theme 2	Theme 3

2 Now take Sue Gaulke's advice and write down three questions you think your audience would be likely to ask about each theme.

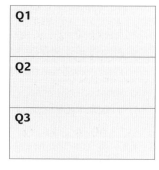

Q1	Q1	Q1
Q2	Q2	Q2
Q3	Q3	Q3

3 Work with a partner. Briefly outline the themes of your presentation to him/her and be prepared to clarify if necessary. Then take the questions one by one plus any follow-up questions your partner may have.

4 Which themes were hardest to explain? Did you lack vocabulary at any point? Which questions were the toughest to answer? Why? What strategies could you have used to handle them better?

5 🔊 2.29 Sometimes, especially in less individualistic cultures, an invitation to ask questions can initially be met with silence! Listen to three speakers trying to deal with this. Whose approach would suit you best?

6 Match the expressions (a–j) opposite to their functions by writing in the corresponding letter. The first one has been done for you as an example.

a You claimed that … . Could you tell us how you arrived at that figure? `e`

b Going back for a moment to what you were saying about … ☐

c But you still haven't answered my question, which is … ☐

d I want to take you up on what you said about … ☐

e You told us … . Do you have any data to support that? ☐

f I think you mentioned … . Could you just elaborate on that? ☐

g OK, then. Well, let me put it another way … ☐

h Oh, OK, fair enough. Point taken. I see what you're saying. ☐

i When you were outlining …, you said … . What exactly did you mean? ☐

j One thing I'm still not clear about. Did you say … or am I mistaken? ☐

Functions

a asking for an explanation

b making a criticism

c referring to an earlier point

d rephrasing a question

e querying a point

f asking for proof

g clearing up a misunderstanding

h pushing for an answer

i conceding a point

j asking for more detail

7 🎧 **2.30** A management consultant has just given a presentation on marketing strategy. Listen to five short exchanges from the Q&A session which followed. Write the functions in **6** in the order you hear the audience members using them. The first one has been done for you as an example.

Extract 1 `c` ☐   Extract 2 ☐ ☐   Extract 3 ☐ ☐   Extract 4 ☐ ☐   Extract 5 ☐ ☐

8 Turn to page 93 to practise fielding questions.

9 As you can see in some of the expressions in **6**, when asking questions at the end of a presentation, it's often useful to set the context before you ask the question.

(*Context*) You claimed that … (*Question*) Can you tell us how you …?

(*Context*) You mentioned … (*Question*) Could you just elaborate on that?

Sometimes you need to set the context in two stages as you zoom in on your question:

(*Context*) When you were outlining … (*Zoom*) you said … (*Question*) What exactly did you mean?

Now turn to page 93 to practise contextualising your questions in this way. You can evaluate your performance using the feedback form on the website.

10 Why do you think it might not be such a good idea to finish your presentation with the Q&A session? See what public speaking pro Tom Antion has to say about it. And good luck in your future presentations!

> Many public speakers make their biggest mistakes during their question and answer sessions. The presenter has a great program, does a powerful close, opens the floor up to questions, answers them well, and then … fades off the stage into oblivion, never to be seen again. OK maybe not that dramatic, but still a big mistake. If you don't have a second powerful close after the Q&A period, it could have a negative impact on your whole presentation. Make sure you have two good closes whenever there is a possibility of a Q&A session.
> *Tom Antion, professional public speaker, AmazingPublicSpeaking.com*

Bringing it all together

{ Congratulations! You've successfully completed the course. Now comes the tricky part – bringing it all together in your own dynamic presentation.
Mark Powell, author of Dynamic Presentations

Choose a presentation (or part of a presentation) you have given in the past or may have to give in the future. Alternatively, select any interesting topic you'd like to be able to talk about. You may find it helpful to start off by mind-mapping some initial ideas.

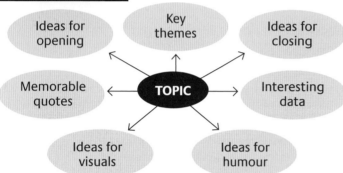

2 Can you reduce your basic message to a single phrase or sentence? You may need to think about this!

Key message:

3 Now sketch out the structure of your presentation using sticky notes, a whiteboard or some other non-digital device. Don't rush this stage.

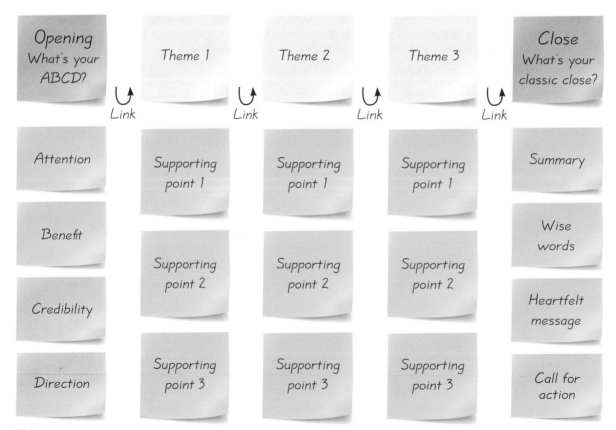

4 Look at the presentation plan you created in **3** and consider the following:

a You know audience attention peaks in the first and last few minutes of your talk. Have you designed a sufficiently powerful opening 'hook'? Are you closing with a 'bang'?

b You can create more peaks of interest throughout your talk by alternating good meaty content with entertaining stories, examples and visuals. This is sometimes referred to as having 'steak and sizzle'. Check your plan. Have you got the right balance? You don't want all steak and no sizzle (dull, heavy content) or all sizzle and no steak (plenty of fun but nothing to say)!

5 As you know, you can add more sizzle by putting key facts and figures into interesting contexts. Have you done this?

6 Add further impact using some of the techniques you've been practising on this course.

| Repetition (words, sounds) | Rhetorical questions | Groups of three (plus one) | Contrasts and opposites | Similes (it's like …) | Metaphors (sport, war, growth, etc.) |

7 Now go to your PowerPoint or Keynote application and design your slides. As you prepare, consider:

a Have you put too much information on any of the slides? If so, cut it down to the essentials or create another slide.

b Have you got attractive, relevant images or just charts and diagrams? Remember to keep your visuals visual.

c Have you chosen the largest font size possible? Don't forget the 10–20–30 rule.

d Have you left yourself anything to say about the slides or do they say everything for you? If you don't want to compete with your visuals, make sure they only tell half the story.

8 When you've got your slides more or less how you want them, run through your presentation a few times with them. If you can, ask someone to listen to you and give you feedback. Your slides should help you to stay on track, but don't use them as notes – you're supposed to know what slide is coming next!

9 You're almost ready! But first, take a few moments to prepare for the kind of questions your audience might ask. Think especially of any difficult questions that could come up. Do you remember how to handle:

- unnecessary questions?
- multiple questions?
- off-topic questions?

You might want to refresh your memory of the D8 system.

10 OK, you're on! Time to give your presentation. You can evaluate your final performance using the feedback form on the website. Good luck!

Deal with
Defuse
Defer
Divide up
Disarm
Define
Deflect
Decline

Audio scripts

Extract 1: What's in a name? If your most valuable asset is your brand, everything. For example, did you know that for over 20 years Apple Computers was locked in a legal dispute with Apple Corps, the holding company owned by The Beatles, over their right to use the Apple name? And did you know that the giant American brewer Anheuser-Busch is still unable to call Budweiser beer 'Budweiser' in Germany and France because that's the registered name belonging to the Budvar brewery in the Czech Republic? Today I want to talk to you about the multi-billion-dollar business of creating and protecting brand identity.

Extract 2: You know, there's a common misconception that mergers just don't work. In fact, we're repeatedly told that 70 to 80% of them fail. And it's true that one of the biggest of all time, the $180 billion AOL Time Warner merger went badly wrong. But that's the thing. It's mega-mergers that fail. When you merge with innovative smaller businesses, it's a different story – particularly in research-intensive industries like yours. Take pharmaceuticals. To date, Pfizer has formed successful alliances with over a thousand biotech start-ups. And in IT Cisco averages one small business acquisition every six weeks. Has it been successful? Well, let's put it this way, Eighteen years after it went public its market capitalisation is bigger than Dell, Xerox and Apple combined!

Extract 3: I'd like to talk to you this morning about data rescue or what to do when your computer goes into meltdown, taking your data with it. So, to start off, could I ask you to raise your hand if you've backed up your hard disc in, oh, let's say, the last week …? Nobody? Right. OK, how about the last month …? Four people, OK. How about ever? A dozen of you. Good, good for you! Backing up your hard disc is a bit like making a dentist appointment, isn't it? We all know we should do it, but we just keep putting it off. Well, the system I'm going to show you today means that you'll never have to back up your data again … and you'll never lose it.

Extract 4: I think it was David Sarnoff, the ex-president of RCA, who said: 'Competition brings out the best in products and the worst in people.' And of no two companies is that more true than of Coke and Pepsi. Between these two soft drinks giants the competition could not be more aggressive. My favourite joke about that is the one about the Pepsi executive who gets called into the boss's office. 'I'm sorry, Doug,' says the boss, 'but I'm going to have to fire you. It's a little embarrassing, but you tested positive for Coke.' OK, we're talking today about what it means to be 'competitive'. So, just for a minute or two, could you turn to a partner and discuss what the word 'competitive' means to you?

Extract 5: As small business owners, you know your number one enemy is cash flow and that you need to keep generating new business to survive. For over a decade, attracting customers has meant having a website and maybe advertising online. But it's hard to know just how effective that is when, according to the latest survey, there are now over 100 million websites out there! How would you like to be able to have someone target potential customers for you, generate sales calls and maximise sales conversion? Just imagine what it would be like to know that for every thousand dollars you invest in sales, you are getting eight to ten times your investment in new business. I work for a company called LeadTracker.com. We do one thing. And we do it well. We get you noticed online.

Extract 1: Ladies and gentlemen, to take this project to the next stage we need your total commitment to the ideas behind it. But we need more than that. We need you to go back to your divisions and units and project teams and become champions for this new initiative, to spread the word and build confidence in the new direction we are about to take. Without you and your people we cannot make this strategy work. Without your actions, it's all just words. We're counting on you to make this happen … Thank you very much.

Extract 2: OK, I'm going to break off in a moment. So let's take a look back at what we've spoken about this morning. We've looked at the five ways a product can fail. First, we looked at extension failures – trying to stretch your brand too far, as Harley Davidson did when it tried to make perfume! We also looked at PR failures and the R.J. Reynolds Joe Camel campaign, marketing cigarettes to young people. Then we looked at cultural failures and KFC in Hong Kong. We moved on to look at people failures at Planet Hollywood and Fashion Café. Finally, we looked at failures of ideas. And it is from these that we can learn the biggest lesson. The list of failed product ideas is almost endless. Kellogg's Cereal Mates, Pepsi AM, the Barbie computer, Clairol's 'Touch of Yoghurt' shampoo – all jokes in their respective industries. But behind each of these spectacular failures was the basis for a brilliant idea. To create future successes we have only to revisit the failures of the past … Thanks very much.

Extract 3: You know, I've been where you are now. I've sat in a six-by-six cubicle with a list of cold leads and a telephone just waiting for me to pick it up and start calling. But in my day it was easier. I can remember when it was just a question of going out there and getting the business. It took dedication, indestructible self-confidence and a lot of hard work, but the business was there to be had. Today, you have to create the business. So, if you take just one thing from this talk today, take this. I used to be a salesman – and a very good one. But you're more than that. You're entrepreneurs, creating business each and every day. For you, the challenges and the opportunities are so much greater. Enjoy the risks you have to take, for with greater risks come greater rewards … Thank you very much.

Extract 4: It was Ricardo Semler, the Brazilian CEO and author of the bestselling *Maverick!,* who said: 'Democracy has yet to penetrate the workplace.' He said: 'There are companies which are prepared to change the way they work. They realise that nothing can be based on what used to be, that there is a better way. But 99% of companies are not ready.

They are caught in a kind of industrial Jurassic Park.' Well said. There are enough dinosaurs in this industry of ours already. If we want to be part of the one percent, we have to evolve. And today's talk has been about how to speed up our evolution ... Thank you.

🎧 Track 1.04
1B Exercise 6

The audio script is in the module: 1B Opening and closing.

🎧 Track 1.05
1B Exercise 7

Speaker: As we go through this morning, I'd like you to be asking yourselves a question. How do you know when you give a presentation that your audience is going to care about what you have to tell them? Well, we'll come back to that later ...

... I started my presentation by asking you all a question. How do you know your audience is going to care about what you tell them? Now, I'm going to answer that question. Before you *tell* them what's in it for *them*, *show* them what's in it for *you*. Show them how much *you* care about it. Enthusiasm is infectious and so is indifference. If it matters to *you*, it will matter to *them* ... Good luck in your future presentations.

🎧 Track 1.06
2A Exercise 4

The audio script is in the module: 2A Smooth structure.

🎧 Track 1.07
2B Exercise 4

Extract 1: They say 'an economist is an expert who'll know *tomorrow* why the things he predicted *yesterday* didn't happen *today*'. The same could be said of most financial advisers.

In the world of investment, it remains a popular misconception that if you want to beat the stock market, you really have to seek professional advice. And people still tend to assume that with the assistance of a professional financial adviser you can't fail to get a better return on your investment.

Wrong. Statistically speaking, two-thirds of City 'experts' underperform the stock market index. In fact, according to some of the latest research, this is a lot less than many amateurs can achieve. In one study, for example, a group of British schoolchildren took part in a stock market simulation game and 80% of them managed to beat the index.

So, in actual fact, a professional adviser might just be the *worst* person to go to for financial advice. For, in reality, 'professional' doesn't mean they're better. It simply means they charge for being worse!

Extract 2: Could I just ask those of you who drive to work to raise your hand if you actually enjoy the experience? Well, don't worry. Help is at hand.

This is the CommuterMate, the motorist's electronic friend. As you can see, it features GPS, which constantly monitors car speed and gives you 1,000 metres' warning of police cameras. It also alerts you to traffic queues and accident hotspots. Plus, it includes free automatic online updates and can be plugged straight into your vehicle's cigarette lighter.

What this means, in a nutshell, is you can set it up in minutes and avoid almost any kind of headache on the road. But the greatest advantage of the CommuterMate is that it has none of the usual reliability problems.

So, how does it measure up to the competition? Well, in terms of cost, it compares very favourably with similar devices because, as I mentioned, the system automatically updates for free. And, as far as reliability is concerned, well, there's really no comparison. The CommuterMate is in a class of its own ...

Extract 3: No one escapes a deep recession – not even the rich. Did you know that in the last 12 months the four hundred richest people in the USA have, between them, lost three hundred billon dollars? Three ... hundred ... billion. That's huge. That's the annual GDP of Hong Kong. Now for the average working man or woman this may not seem like a big deal. But in the luxury car industry it's a full-scale catastrophe!

The global economic downturn we are currently suffering has hit us hard. Throughout the industry we are seeing major production slowdowns with the expectation of a sustained fall in demand. And here at Mirage we are increasingly vulnerable to competition at the lower end of the luxury sector. Does this cloud have a silver lining? I think it does. The fact that brands like BMW are seeing an increase in sales proves that there is, most definitely, still a market for luxury, but affordable luxury. The challenge for us, then, is to make the luxury products we offer more affordable, but no less luxurious.

What this means is: we need to be introducing better payment plans, trade-in deals and preferential rates for insurance policies. I want to see us doing everything we can to make the dream of owning a Mirage Turbo a practical reality for the customers we traditionally attract.

🎧 Track 1.08
2B Exercise 7

Speaker: I read an article in *Businessweek* the other day entitled: 'How many management problems turn out to be people problems?' The writer, who spent eight years at the World Bank, seemed to think it's pretty much all of them. And I agree with him. *All* problems are *people* problems. In IT, with our heads stuck in computer manuals, I think we sometimes lose sight of that.

As you know, over the last six months we've been having problems with the introduction of new computer technology throughout the company. Basically, the main difficulty has been getting the different departments to adopt the new system. Another related problem, I think, has been a certain lack of respect between the operational and IT divisions. Poor communication has also compounded the problem. We're simply not talking to each other. And we need to fix that.

So, what are the options? Well, one option would simply be to make full use of the new technology mandatory across all departments. Another alternative would be to set up a forum for members of different divisions to decide how best to implement the technology. Most ambitiously, it's been suggested that we should replace the current divisional structure of the company with a more integrated structure consisting of cross-functional teams.

Because of the cost and complexity of a corporate restructuring exercise, I think we can eliminate that last option right away. And we don't think simply issuing a directive is going to address the real problem. So we can rule out that option as well. In our view, our best option is to create a Knowledge Management forum, a platform for discussion. But what will this involve?

Well, our first priority is to get buy-in from everyone in the company. Once we've sorted that out, then we can decide what form that forum should take – face-to-face, online or both? And, finally, what's needed is to set up a dedicated intranet, arrange KM workshops, information-sharing sessions and so on. Let's look at these in more detail …

💿 **Track 1.09**
3A Exercise 2

The audio script is in the module: 3A Voice power.

💿 **Track 1.10**
3A Exercises 4 and 6

The audio script is in the module: 3A Voice power.

💿 **Track 1.11**
3B Exercise 1

Version 1: OK, um, I'd like you to look at this chart, which, er, shows consumer response to the campaign over the, erm, over the last six months. And, er, oh, wait a minute. Er, yeah, here we are. Er, so, as you can see, overall, er, the response has been, you know, very positive, er, really. I mean, fifty-nine percent, er, yeah, fifty-nine percent said they'd tried the product and, of those, of those fifty-nine percent, er, about half said they actually preferred it to their, er, usual brand. So, you know, we're like, er, really pleased with that result.

Version 2: OK. I'd like you to look at this chart, which shows consumer response to the campaign over the last six months. … As you can see, overall, the response has been very positive. Fifty-nine percent said they'd tried the product and, of those fifty-nine percent, about half said they actually preferred it to their usual brand. So we're really pleased with that result.

💿 **Track 1.12**
3B Exercise 4

The audio script is in the module: 3B Voice power.

💿 **Track 1.13**
3B Exercise 6

The audio script is in the module: 3B Voice power.

💿 **Track 1.14**
4A Exercise 3

Italian: Well, what can I say? I'm Italian. For us good design is a way of life. Actually, for me, neither of these

two slides is very beautiful, but the first certainly has a lot of power. I like the use of black and the panoramic photograph. Most important, it makes a point – one point, the key point, which is, look, the market for 3D eyewear is going to be huge. And that's all the audience needs to know. The rest the presenter can mention in support of their main point. But the audience doesn't need to see it.

Dutch: Well, first of all, I think you have to ask: what is the purpose of the visual aid? The first slide is obviously trying to get your attention. And it does. But it doesn't tell you very much. In the Netherlands we like to see a little more data, more figures. In the second slide, which is also quite attractive, I think, everything is itemised. And I actually prefer to see all the details while I'm listening to a presentation. I don't want to have questions in my mind when I'm trying to concentrate.

Swedish: In Sweden we also like to have all the necessary information, but that needn't mean bad design. The problem with the second slide is that it has too many bullet points and far too many words per line. An audience can't read and listen at the same time. The background makes it difficult to read too. The first slide is clever because it makes you wonder what the speaker's point is going to be. A good visual should make you think 'Wow! What's he going to tell us about this?' A bad one makes you think 'I wish he'd just shut up and let me read!'

Japanese: In general, Japanese prefer simple design, so the first slide is the clear winner here. But I have to admit that many Japanese find it quite difficult to understand Western presenters, so, to be honest, the more information they can read, the better. The second slide may be a little dense, but it will be appreciated by a Japanese audience. As a speaker, it can also be useful to have more information on your slides to help you remember what to say, use them as notes. But I suppose that's a bad thing. Your slides are supposed to be for your audience, not you!

💿 **Track 1.15**
4A Exercise 6

Speaker 1: For me, the master of using props in a presentation would have to be Apple's Steve Jobs. I remember when Apple introduced the MacBook

Air as the world's thinnest notebook computer. Steve said it was so thin you could put it in an ordinary office envelope. The audience laughed. So he went to the side of the stage, picked up an office envelope and proceeded to open it. And inside, sure enough, there it was – the MacBook Air, thin as a company report. Just brilliant.

Speaker 2: Yeah, I remember that speech … Erm, have any of you ever heard of a conference called the TED conference? No? Fantastic event. It's business, science and technology mostly. In fact, you can watch some of the speeches online if you want to. Anyway, one year there was this brain scientist called Jill Bolte Taylor talking about what it feels like to be actually having a stroke, because she'd had one herself. And suddenly someone brings on a human brain in a jar of fluid, a real one, and she takes it out and starts talking about it. And you can hear the effect it has on the audience, but she certainly got everyone's attention!

Speaker 3: Ugh, sounds gross to me! Er, the best use of a prop I've seen is probably when John Chambers, the CEO of Cisco, was presenting a new experimental version of the TelePresence system. TelePresence is this really advanced teleconferencing system. And, er, the new version will mean that people in different parts of the world will all be able to attend the same meeting as holograms! Yeah, I know, it sounds like science fiction. But that's exactly what he did. He actually invited two colleagues on stage with him and they were 3D holograms! It was like something out of *Star Trek*.

Speaker 4: Yeah, I've seen that presentation on video. It's pretty cool. But going back to Steve Jobs for a minute, he's given so many great presentations. But my favourite is the one where he introduced the first iPod Nano back in 2005. Remember? He'd been talking about the iPod and the iPod Mini and how well they fit in your standard pocket. Then the camera zooms in on him and he points to that little pocket jeans have inside the main pocket, you know the one? And he asks the audience: 'Ever wondered what *this* pocket is for?' And everybody laughs because, you know, they're thinking, yeah, what *is* that pocket for? And then Jobs takes the Nano out of that pocket and says: 'Well, now we know.' Pure genius!

Speaker: Good morning. Thanks for coming. The title of my talk this morning is *What Women Want*. And I'm going to be asking the age-old question: Are women different from men? More particularly, do they behave differently when they are buying? And, if so, should we be marketing to them in a different way?

Well, I can tell you straight away: yes, they *are* different. Yes, they *do* buy differently. And, yes, we *should* be marketing to them in a *totally* different way. Unfortunately, 90% of businesses are totally useless at doing so.

So, first off, let's be clear. Women spend billions of dollars! Many more billions than men. And yet, so far, marketers, most of them men, have failed to take any account at all of women's phenomenal consumer spending power.

Have a look at this. This diagram represents the total number of households. And, as you can see, according to research carried out by the National Foundation for Women Business Owners, women are the primary decision-makers for consumer goods in 85% of them. 85%! The figures speak for themselves. But let's take a closer look. You'll notice that in those households women influence eight out of ten purchasing decisions. In eight out of ten cases, the woman decides, yes or no, whether to buy. And I'm not just talking groceries here. I'm talking furnishings, vacations, savings plans, cars. Just about anything that doesn't have a remote control! I should point out that when it comes to big purchases like a new home, their influence is slightly reduced – women make just 75% of real-estate decisions!

I'd also like to draw your attention to these figures, published by the Internet Marketing Association. Obviously, we might expect women to be spending more at the shopping mall. But what about online? Surely, that's still a male domain? Not any more. These figures show that on average women are also spending 10% more than men over the Internet. Now, let's put that into perspective. It means that on the biggest day for web sales this year, women spent $70 million more than men. So the real question is what *don't* women buy?

Now, what are the implications of this? Simply, that if you're not marketing directly to women in a way that women want to be marketed to, you just lost your company three-quarters of its revenue this year. For all the wrong reasons, men may on average still be earning more than women, but they are not the ones spending most of what they earn.

So, what are the main differences in buying behaviour between men and women? Let me talk you through them one by one …

French: I work in R&D for a pharmaceutical company in Paris. And in our line of business there's a protocol for how we must present at international congresses. First, our presentations are very short – maybe only ten or fifteen minutes. And in that time we have to cover a lot of data. If we miss out just one thing, you can be sure in the question-and-answer session, someone will raise the matter. Unfortunately, this does mean that many of our presentations are rather information-heavy. We have a million slides. For us, data is our only defence against the audience! But I think that is inevitable in a highly competitive, high-tech industry such as ours.

British: Erm, well, I work for a PR company in Manchester. So, for me, presentations are all part of the job. I started out as a journalist, so I'm used to editing my own work. Because, well, with figures, if you throw too many at the audience, you may as well have none. I mean, if you want to make the kind of statements at a press conference that are going to become front-page news, then you have to stick to the two or three facts you really want people to remember. That means missing a lot out, because if you want people to get the message, you can't make it too simple.

Chinese: I work for a multinational bank in Shanghai, so I'm quite used to attending presentations by American and German colleagues. It's interesting. Americans generally stick to the *key* figures. Germans want to show you *all* the figures. Germans seem to be very focused on the present situation. Americans are more short-term future-oriented. For them it's all about

meeting their next quarterly targets. But we take a broader perspective. For us, past performance is as important as present and future performance. So, yes, I suppose we do like quite a lot of statistical background.

The audio script is in the Key (page 67).

The audio script is in the Key (page 67).

a Globally, 256 million people are involved in start-ups. To put that into perspective, if they joined hands, they'd circle the world 12 times!

b The world consumes 164.5 billion litres of bottled water a year. To give you an idea of just how much that is, it's enough to fill Loch Ness 22 times!

c The world's richest 1½% are worth around $50 trillion. That means they currently control just over half the planet's wealth!

d Apple's Fifth Avenue megastore turns over $350 million a year. That's roughly the equivalent of selling 10,000 Mercedes-Benz cars!

Speaker: Have a look at this chart, which shows the extra amount of leisure time enjoyed by men in comparison with women in 12 different countries. I'm sure it'll come as no surprise to most of you here today that right across the globe men do seem to have a lot more spare time on their hands, whilst 'a woman's work is' quite literally 'never done'!

Italian men have by far the best deal with nearly 80 minutes a day more leisure than their female counterparts. Norwegians fare the worst, getting just a few extra minutes. But let's put that in perspective. Even just three minutes a day is around 18 hours of free time a year – an extra weekend of putting your feet up!

Perhaps predictably, the Latin countries – Spain at well over three quarters of an hour and France at a little over half an hour – tend to come higher up the chart. And Germany and

Sweden at just over twenty minutes nearer the bottom.

But the real surprise is the figure for Poland. On average, men here have almost an hour a day more than women to take a nap or 'veg out' in front of the TV. Over a typical week, that's enough time to watch four Hollywood movies! It's also equivalent to an extra night's sleep!

🎵 Track 1.22
5B Exercise 8

Speaker: The advertisement had an immediate impact. In January our CT rate went up by 2½% from just ½% to 3% – an amazing six-fold increase! Then in February we saw a drop of 1¾ to just 1¼%. But that's still well above average. In March the figure fluctuated between a high of 2 and a low of 1%. Finally, in April it hovered around 1½% to finish up at a little over that by the end of the campaign. All in all, an excellent response!

🎵 Track 1.23
6A Exercise 2

a Well, in Brazil I think you have to have a little bit of theatre when you give a presentation. We like people to be, you know, dynamic – especially if you are presenting to a young audience. You can do the whole rock-and-roll thing with them! Lots of jumping around! With older, more conservative audiences, it's probably better to be just a little calmer, not quite so extrovert, but still, you know, animated.

b Erm, I think most Australians appreciate a direct, no-nonsense approach. I mean, you should certainly be friendly and all that, but if you're selling, it's OK to sell quite hard, as long as you don't come across as arrogant. We don't like that. So my advice is to be natural, be genuine. Humour's always welcome, but don't try to put on a special show. Make sure your body language flows naturally from your words, not the other way round.

c Er, well, in Finland, we don't like the Hollywood style of presenting too much. We prefer a good honest approach really. I mean, we don't want you to be boring, but good content should speak for itself. So, not too loud, not too extrovert. That makes us nervous. Keep everything simple when you present to a Finnish audience. And don't forget the one

bit of body language that works wherever you go in the world – a smile!

d In the Gulf we like presenters who speak with passion. Speaking well, with lots of eye contact, firm gestures – these are the things that impress us. I have many Western colleagues who are uncomfortable with this, but I explain it this way. In private conversation we sit close to each other and are very tactile. In public speaking you must close the distance between you and your audience by increasing the volume of your voice and all your movements. That way we know you are sincere and confident, someone to be trusted.

🎵 Track 1.24
6B Exercise 7

a OK, so the first thing is: watch what you do with your hands. Apart from your face, your hands are the things your audience is going to notice the most. Now, it doesn't really matter how much you use your hands when you speak as long as you do use them. But remember to vary your gestures. You see some speakers using the same gesture over and over again. And that really is distracting. The audience can't concentrate on what you're saying because they're just thinking: 'I wonder if he's going to do that thing again? Oh, yes, there he goes!' So fix the 'hands problem' first.

b I've seen some speakers try to fix the 'hands problem' by folding their arms. They think it makes them look relaxed. It doesn't. It makes them look defensive and creates a barrier between them and their audience. Same thing with a podium. Another barrier. If you fold your arms, you're trapped. You can't move your hands. If you stand behind a podium, you're trapped. You can hardly move at all. The solution to the 'podium trap' is to insist on having a radio mike, get out from behind that damn podium and to hell with the conference organisers! They don't have to give your talk. You do.

c Objects make a 'hands problem' ten times worse. Clicking pens, adjusting ties, playing with jewellery, fiddling with your shirt cuffs, rattling change in your pockets – all guaranteed to make you look nervous and annoy your audience. So empty your

pockets before you start, don't wear dangly, noisy jewellery, put pens away and leave items of clothing alone! They look fine as they are. And if they don't, it's too late now.

d The problem with nerves is that they tend to make you become hyperactive and move around too much. You've got all this nervous energy you're trying to get rid of, so you pace around, up and down, back and forth. Stop it. It's making the audience exhausted just looking at you! Relax. Take it easy. It's not the 100 metres. Having said take it easy, I've also got to say don't take it *too* easy. If you're standing there with your hands in your pockets or on your hips and a lazy grin on your face, you're going to look much too casual. Get the balance right. Move, stop, stand still, move again. And focus on your audience, not yourself.

🎵 Track 2.02
7A Exercise 2

The audio script is in the Key (page 70).

🎵 Track 2.03
7A Exercise 3

a This isn't really so surprising, is it?
b But we won't let this stop us, will we?
c We certainly can't complain, can we?
d We've been here before, haven't we?
e I said it was good news, didn't I?
f You know what's going to happen, don't you?

🎵 Track 2.04
7A Exercise 4

a Shouldn't we be focusing our attention on our core business?
b Offshoring – isn't this something we need to be looking at?
c Isn't it time we started to take internet advertising seriously?
d Haven't we had enough of being number two in this industry?
e Isn't there a need for more accountability at board level?
f Aren't we in danger of losing some of our best customers?

🎵 Track 2.05
7A Exercise 5

Speaker: Let's just talk about email for a moment. If you're anything like me, you probably wish email had never been invented! I mean, I don't know about you, but on a typical day

I probably waste more time on email than just about anything else. And it's not just spam, is it? When was the last time you received dozens of emails that didn't even directly concern you? Raise your hand if that's happened to you … Right. I think that's something we can all relate to. Email is inescapable.

So, what if I was to say to you that email, as we know it, is dead; that email will soon be as obsolete as the fax machine? You'd think I was crazy, right? I mean, there are currently 1.7 billion email users out there! But let me ask you a question. How many of you pay regular visits to sites like Facebook, MySpace or Twitter? How about texting? Most of you. Interesting. If, like me, you find yourself more and more involved in social networking these days, then you should already know that email is on its way out.

But let me share some statistics with you. Did you know that 300 million users spend 8 billion minutes a day just on Facebook? And would it surprise you to learn that students now hardly use email at all – except to contact professors and parents! Now, I know what you're thinking. You're thinking, well, OK, sure, we know kids are the biggest users of Web 2.0 technology and texting. But, you see, that's where you'd be wrong. The fastest-growing group of social networkers is actually women over 35. And the biggest markets for SMS are China and India. The Chinese alone send half a trillion text messages a year! And you don't need me to tell you that, together, China, India and women over 35 exercise a tremendous amount of influence!

Track 2.06
7B Exercise 3

a You know, I don't think you necessarily have to *say* anything funny to get a laugh. There are a lot of other things you can do. In fact, visual humour often crosses cultural boundaries better. I remember seeing Steve Jobs presenting the iPhone back in 2007. It was a superb presentation. You could see the audience getting more and more excited, but he kept them waiting and waiting as he talked them through the history of Apple's past successes: the Macintosh, the iPod and so on. Finally, he announced it. 'And today', he said, 'today Apple is going to reinvent the phone! And here it is …' And up on the screen there's this enormous picture of a first-generation iPod with an old-fashioned telephone dial stuck on it. Big laugh! What a fantastic use of a visual aid to tell the joke for you!

b I think humour can save a lot of potentially embarrassing situations. For example, getting people in the audience to talk to each other at the beginning of your presentation can be a good way to get them thinking about your subject. But sometimes people are reluctant to do it. I saw Fons Trompenaars – you know, the intercultural guru, very funny speaker – I saw him avoid this problem really well in a talk he gave once. He started off by inviting people in the audience to talk to their neighbour about their own definition of culture – you know, what does culture mean for *you*? 'Talk to your neighbour,' he said. They looked back at him. 'If you're sitting on your own, talk to yourself. As long as you make noise, it's fine.' That got a laugh and, more importantly, people started to talk to each other.

c I agree that the right joke at the right moment can rescue a lot of difficult situations. And it doesn't even have to be very funny. I once saw a speaker … she was right in the middle of her talk when pow! All the electricity went off! Now, we were in a kind of lecture hall, so it was completely dark. And, of course, none of the audio-visual equipment would work. I felt really sorry for her. But she handled the situation brilliantly. She came to the front of the platform and said: 'I was going to show you a really interesting PowerPoint slide. But there doesn't seem to be any power … so what's the point?' And everybody laughed. And right then you could see the relief in the audience as they're thinking: It's going to be OK, she can see the funny side.

d No matter whether you're going to use humour or not, I think it's usually a good idea to at least start off with something that gets a bit of a laugh. A few years ago I was at an IT conference in the States and I attended a talk by a guy called Mohanbir Sawhney. He's a professor at the Kellogg School of Management – brilliant guy. Now Sawhney's a Sikh, so he always wears a turban. So on he comes in a bright pink turban and tie. Immediately gets the audience's attention. 'Happy Valentine's Day,' he says, 'I thought I'd brand myself pink to be consistent with the occasion.' And the audience loves it, because it's so unexpected. But that's what's clever. Because, of course, Sawhney knows one of the first things people notice about him is his turban. And that's what makes the joke work.

e All good 'spontaneous' remarks in presentations are actually prepared in advance. The secret is to make them sound spontaneous when you deliver them. One speaker I really like – and he's a master of this – is the educationalist and creativity expert, Sir Ken Robinson. He's always very funny in that casual British way. Never uses visual aids at all – just chats to his audience. Tells lots of stories. Anyway, the last time I saw him, he was the very last speaker on the conference programme. It was the closing address. And that's always a difficult job because everyone's exhausted by that stage. So Sir Ken, he knows this, of course, and he anticipates the problem. 'I am the last speaker,' he says, 'I am the only thing standing between *you* … and going home.' And, naturally, there are lots of laughs because that's exactly what everyone was thinking before he came on!

Track 2.07
7B Exercise 5

Extract 1: OK, we're going to pass around some working models of the device for you to have a look at, so you can get a feel for how it works. Now, there aren't as many devices as there are people, so perhaps you could share in groups of three or four.

Extract 2: If you look at the slide, you'll see there's a puzzle we sometimes use to test thinking styles. What you have to do is connect the boxes in such a way that the numbers on the sides you connect all add up to ten. Simple, yes? Or maybe not so simple! Try this on your own first.

Extract 3: Now, we've been talking about 'brand royalty' – the idea that some brands are just so strong, they form part of our mental landscape. But I can see some of you are sceptical. So, I'm just going to play three or four seconds of five different pieces of music from television commercials and for each one I want you to write down the first product or service that comes into your head. OK?

Extract 4: OK, you should all have a copy of the handout. So can you just work with the person sitting either directly in front of or behind you to fill it in? I'll give you about ten minutes for this, OK? Great, thanks.

Extract 5: OK, I'm going to put some statistics up on the screen. You'll find a full set of figures in the report, but these are just the key data. And I'd like you to decide what conclusions *you* think we can draw from them.

Extract 6: Now, as you know, as part of our market research, we conducted interviews in our stores with customers in the 35 to 49 age bracket. And these were filmed for later analysis. You've seen the results in the report. So, we'll just run the video and then there'll be time for questions.

Extract 7: If you look on the card you were given, you'll find some instructions, yes? Good. So, I'd like you to get up and find the person with the same instructions as you and then see if you can carry out those instructions together. All right? Good luck!

Extract 8: Now, I think that's quite enough background from me. Let's go online and see the new site. And maybe we could try this out together. If you shout out the things you want to see, I'll do the clicking! OK?

🔘 Track 2.08
8A Exercise 2

a It's not a question of qualifications. It's a question of talent.
b I always say total quality begins with total commitment.
c What's the use of setting goals if your goals are unrealistic?
d One thing we don't need is more data. We're drowning in data as it is!
e A decline in the market doesn't have to mean a decline in sales as well.
f We're still running at zero profit. But, from zero the only way is up.

🔘 Track 2.09
8A Exercise 3

a First of all, I'm pleased to report that profits are up … up by 38%.
b It's a cliché, I know, but this firm has always … always put its people first.
c Ladies and gentlemen, it's time … time to face the facts.
d So, that's what happened – what I want to know is why … why did we let it happen?

e What's really … really important for us to do right now is this …
f One thing I know: we must never … never again lose our sense of focus.
g Nobody … nobody likes failure, but some people are more afraid of success.
h We've come a long … long way to get to where we are today.
i And today … today we're announcing our biggest breakthrough ever.

🔘 Track 2.10
8A Exercise 4

a Nowhere have we been more successful than in South America – nowhere.
b No one has ever been able to beat us on price – no one.
c Everyone in the beta test was positive about the product – everyone.
d Nothing is beyond us if we work together as a team – nothing.
e Anything would be better than the system we've got at the moment – anything.
f Everything in this market is about to change – everything.

🔘 Track 2.11
8A Exercise 7

a Properly priced, packaged and promoted, this product cannot fail.
b China is not our main market, but it may be a major market in the future.
c Of course, this is a serious problem to which there's no simple solution.
d In the world of international finance this firm remains a formidable force.
e I know that if we work together as a team we can take on the competition.
f If we cannot challenge change, then we have no choice but to embrace it.
g If we don't manage to break even on this by Q4, we may even go bust.

🔘 Track 2.12
8A Exercise 8

The audio script is in the Key (page 72).

🔘 Track 2.13
8B Exercise 4

a So, what's the main challenge we face? The main challenge is piracy. Now what can we do about that?
b So, what's the answer? The answer is viral marketing. But what do I mean by that?

c So, what's the problem? The problem is converting leads into sales. Now how can we improve that?
d So, where are the best opportunities? The best opportunities are in China. But didn't we know that already?
e So, what's my point? My point is that big-budget advertising simply doesn't work. So, what are the alternatives?
f So, what's the plan? The plan is to give our project teams more autonomy. But what will this mean in practice?

🔘 Track 2.14
8B Exercise 5

a We've tripled revenues in two years. So, how did we do it?
b The whole of central Asia is one big golden opportunity. So, what are we waiting for?
c We poured millions into this venture and it flopped. So, where did we go wrong?
d When the patents run out on this product, our competitors will legally be able to clone it. So, what are we going to do about it?
e We spend fifty million dollars a year on internet advertising alone. But how much of that is wasted?
f It's by far the most cost-effective system on the market. So, why isn't it selling?
g In spite of offering excellent salaries and benefits, we're still failing to retain key personnel. So, where do we go from here?
h Retooling the plants is not going to be cheap. So, what sort of figure are we talking about?
i We've considerably stepped up R&D activity. So, how soon can we expect to see results?

🔘 Track 2.15
8B Exercise 8

a What will it take to achieve our goals? Time, effort and tenacity. But, above all, talent.
b How do we plan to become a more socially responsible firm? Through our total commitment to clean energy, sustainability and fair trade. But, most of all, through our commitment to people.
c Where do our key markets lie? In Canada, Russia and Scandinavia. But, first and foremost, Germany.

Track 2.16
8B Exercise 9

Speaker: Traditionally, marketers have always made it their mission to concentrate on 18 to 44-year-olds. After all, this is certainly the sector of the market that's the most fashion-conscious, the most media-aware and the most comfortable with technology. If I can be cynical for a moment, it's also by far the most responsive to advertising.

But in concentrating on the 18 to 44-year-olds, marketers have tended to neglect the so-called 'baby boomers'. Big mistake. Baby boomers, as you know, are the generation born between 1946 and 1964. Many of them are now over 60. Did you know that in the US the over-60s now represent 20 percent of the population – up from 12 percent just over half a century ago? Did you know that there are now more Italians over the age of 60 than under the age of 20? And did you know that by 2050 a phenomenal 40 percent of Japanese will also be over 60? Now, these over-60s have a huge disposable income. They have a large amount of free time in which to spend it. And an increasing amount of lifetime in which to spend it!

But it's not just the over-60s. In the USA households headed by the over-40s represent a staggering 99 percent of the nation's net worth! Makes you wonder if the 18 to 44-year-olds are worth targeting at all!

Now, boomers don't want to be treated like big kids. But they don't want to be treated like geriatrics either. They know they're getting older, but that doesn't mean they have to 'get old'. So, where are the business opportunities? Well, for boomer-oriented brands there are big opportunities in travel and tourism, in adventure holidays and in luxury vehicles. There are big opportunities in health and fitness, in cosmetic and in transplant surgery. There's a boom in the number of boomers and the thing to remember is that boomers want experiences they missed first time round.

Track 2.17
8C Exercise 1

a This year we're number two in the market. This time next year, we'll be number one.

b As they say, it's not a matter of doing things right. It's a matter of doing the right things.

c I'm not asking you to say yes today. I'm asking you not to say no.

d I'm not saying it's a good option. I'm saying it's our only option.

e They say you should look before you leap. I say leap, then look.

f Five years ago we had an idea. Today it has become a reality.

g If we don't seize this opportunity, someone else will.

h We may never be the biggest, but we can still be the best.

Track 2.18
8C Exercise 4

The audio script is in the Key (page 72).

Track 2.19
8D Exercise 5

The audio scripts are in the module: 8D Impact techniques – from Shooting Fish, Wall Street, Thank You for Smoking.

Track 2.20
8D Exercise 6

The audio scripts are in the module: 8D Impact techniques – at Comdex Computer Expo and Stanford University.

Track 2.21
9A Exercise 4

The audio script is in the Key (page 75).

Track 2.22
9A Exercise 6

Speaker 1: Well, I guess you already knew Argentinians like talking! And we like stories. For me, when I present, a story is the best bridge between me and my audience. It's like turning your experience into a movie that the audience can play inside their heads, you know? But the story must be fresh and original. Never use those books of jokes and funny stories you can buy. Be genuine. Watch your audience. Keep your stories personal. And short!

Speaker 2: Well, now, I come from Ireland and one thing people do say about the Irish is that they can tell a good story. Funny stories are always popular, of course. But you don't have to be funny. I mean, if you tell a joke, people expect to get a laugh at the end. So if nobody laughs, it's a disaster. But with a story it doesn't have to get a big laugh – a simple smile will do.

Speaker 3: In China we have a tradition of telling stories to make important points. But I would say that the story should be quite simple and easy to follow. Western humour may not always work with us. It is OK to make a small joke about yourself, but be careful. Do not make jokes about your area of know-how. We want to listen to an expert, not a clown!

Speaker 4: Russians love stories. So, if you think we'll have objections to your ideas, tell us a story. It's like the Trojan Horse, you know? You slip your message inside the story and we accept it. Russians are, how can I say, sometimes suspicious of foreign ideas and especially suspicious of change. But you should know we are also a sentimental and passionate people. And if your story touches us, we can be persuaded.

Track 2.23
9B Exercise 3

a I have a confession to make. The only reason I started my business in the first place is because I failed to get into law school. At the time I was devastated. All my life I'd wanted to be a lawyer. Now I see that failure brought me success. In my first year in business I had the good fortune to be featured in a TV programme about entrepreneurs under the age of 25. I can still remember the film crew coming into my apartment and saying: 'Amy, we'd like to film you in your headquarters.' I said: 'That's great … well, here we are!' Then they said: 'OK, well, we thought we'd film you in a staff meeting or something.' I said: 'Would you excuse me for a minute?' Then I went and phoned all my friends at work and said: 'Can you get over to my apartment right now and pretend to be my employees?' And here we are, just three years later, and most of them *are* my employees and I actually have a headquarters!

b Talking of customer satisfaction, several years ago I used to work for a well-known chain of hotels in Argentina. And, of course, one of the things we used to do was leave a guest satisfaction questionnaire in people's rooms on the day they checked out. Now, as you know, most people don't even bother to fill those questionnaires in. But here's the thing. We noticed that more than half the people who did fill them in and said they were *very* satisfied with their hotel also said 'But I don't plan to return' and 'No, I wouldn't recommend it to somebody else.' Curious, no? And, even more curious, a quarter of those who said they were *dissatisfied* with their hotel returned! Which just goes to show that satisfaction is not the same thing as loyalty. Ask yourself: how would you prefer your life partner to be? Satisfied? ... Or loyal? But seriously, I think we focus far too much on customer satisfaction, when what we should really be focusing on is customer loyalty.

c A few months ago I hit forty and decided I really needed to get fit. Believe it or not, I was once quite an athlete, but, as you can see, I've fallen rather badly out of shape. So I hunted out my old racquet and joined my local tennis club. Now, having not played in almost twenty years I thought I'd better have some lessons. So I went along and joined the advanced class, thinking, well, I used to be pretty good, I'm sure I'll pick it up again quite quickly ... I was terrible! The instructor said: 'No, no, no, you're holding the racquet all wrong.' I said: 'But this is how I was taught to hold it.' He said: 'Oh, dear. I think you'd better join the intermediate class.' So I went to the intermediate class and the instructor said: 'You've acquired a lot of bad habits. Nobody serves like that any more. Why don't you try the beginners' class for a few weeks?' You can imagine my humiliation ... Well, with the beginners I did a little better. I was the second-best player in the class! What was happening? The same thing that often happens when we take on employees with years of experience, but none of it recent. They often need more training than new recruits straight out of university – because they have so much to *unlearn*.

💿 Track 2.24
9B Exercise 5

a She looked up from her desk and said [angrily]: 'What do you want?'
b He said [cheerfully]: 'To be honest, I don't know the first thing about computers.'
c He said [abruptly]: 'Don't interrupt me when I'm speaking!'
d I said [laughingly]: 'You've got to be joking!'
e She took me to one side and said [whispering secretively]: 'I have some

information you might be interested in.'
f He said [officiously]: 'I'm afraid that's not my job.'
g She said [sarcastically]: 'Of course, you're the world's expert on customer relations, aren't you?'
h He said [yelling]: 'I can't hear myself think!'

💿 Track 2.25
9B Exercise 6

Speaker: So I come out into the arrivals area at Charles de Gaulle airport and there's nobody waiting for me. I wait for about quarter of an hour, but still nobody comes. So I ring their office, but there's no answer. And I'm thinking to myself: 'This is very odd.' Another 45 minutes go by. And now I'm really starting to panic. I mean, what am I supposed to do? I'm in a strange city. I don't know a soul. I don't even know which hotel they've booked me into – nothing. Finally – I've almost given up hope by this stage – this tall blonde woman comes up to me and says: 'Are you Dr White?' And I say: 'Yes, I am. Where on earth have you been? I was beginning to think you'd forgotten me.' And she says: 'I'm very sorry! I was held up in traffic.' It's not a great excuse, but, anyway, to cut a long story short, we get into a taxi and head into town, when suddenly she turns to me and says: 'I'm really honoured to be working with one of America's top neurosurgeons!' And I say: 'But I'm not a neurosurgeon. I'm an automotive engineer!' And she says: 'But aren't you Dr White from New York Hospital?' And I say: 'I'm afraid not. I'm Dr White from Cleveland Trucks.' She'd picked up the wrong Dr White!

💿 Track 2.26
10A Exercise 2

a

Speaker 1: To be honest, I just concentrate on sticking to my plan and giving a good presentation! If I start answering questions in the middle of my talk, I may get completely lost! So I usually ask people to leave their questions until the end – or even write them down on cards for me. That way I can have a quick look at them before I answer.

Speaker 2: Actually, for me it's the other way round. I'm more comfortable doing the Q&A. It's more like just having a conversation. So I always invite the audience to ask questions as

we go along. And if they don't ask, I ask *them*! What do *they* think? It's a good way of involving them right from the start.

b

Speaker 1: I think it's very important that everybody gets to *hear* the question. So if there are more than a dozen people in the room, I always repeat it before I answer. I don't ask them if they heard the question. That's like saying the person who asked it should have spoken up! I just go ahead and repeat it.

Speaker 2: Hmm, well, that's OK as long as it isn't a negative or hostile question. If someone asks: 'Why is your system so difficult to use?', you don't want to be repeating 'Why is our system so difficult to use?' You want to remove the value judgement and say something like: 'So, you're asking about the system interface.'

c

Speaker 1: If someone asks a good question, I always thank them for it. It may seem a bit false and unnecessary to compliment someone on their question. But they like it – and at least you've made one friend in the audience! A good question is one that helps you give your presentation better. Maybe it's about something you meant to mention, but forgot. So why not thank the questioner for reminding you?

Speaker 2: Yeah, OK, but what if the next question you get is *not* one you were hoping for? What are you going to say *then*? 'Well, I won't thank you for *your* question'? Don't comment on the questions you get. Just answer them!

d

Speaker 1: If a question is clearly off-topic, I mean really pretty irrelevant, I think you've got to politely point out that it raises a different issue and move on. Otherwise, you're just wasting the rest of your audience's time.

Speaker 2: Hmm, unless it's a totally dumb question, I'd answer it briefly, anyway. *You* may think it's irrelevant, but it may not be. Certainly, the person who asked it thinks it's relevant. And that person could turn out to be important!

e

Speaker 1: If you don't know the answer to a question, admit it. Offer to find out or ask other people in the room what *they* think. Ask the *questioner* what they think. But don't bluff. An audience always knows if you're bluffing. Admitting you don't know will win their respect.

Speaker 2: Well, that may work in your country. In my country you should never admit to not knowing something you're supposed to be an expert in. So I say, if you get a question you can't answer, turn it into a question you *can* answer. The questioner may notice you haven't really answered their question. But nobody else will. It works for politicians!

f

Speaker 1: What do you do when someone asks you a question you've already answered? That's a difficult one. You don't want to say: 'I've already answered that!' But you don't want your audience to think you forgot to mention it either. I usually just briefly refer back to the slide I used earlier.

Speaker 2: But then you make the person who asked the question look as if they weren't paying attention the first time! No, I think you should just briefly answer the question again.

g

Speaker 1: Sometimes someone asks two or three questions at the same time and so I think you've got to first of all break down the questions and then briefly deal with them one at a time.

Speaker 2: But that can take too long and leave no time for other people to ask *their* questions. And you might forget what the second and third questions were while you're answering the first! I think it's better to identify the most important question they've asked and just deal with that.

h

Speaker 1: If the information you're asked for is confidential, say so. Say 'I'm afraid I'm not at liberty to talk about that at this stage' or 'Our legal department has advised me not to discuss that' or 'That's classified information at this point.'

Speaker 2: I think that sounds a little evasive. Make a joke of it if you can. Say something like 'That information is so secret, they haven't even told me' or 'If I told you, I'd have to shoot you.'

🎧 Track 2.27
10A Exercise 6

The audio script is in the key (page 76).

🎧 Track 2.28
10A Exercise 7

The audio script is in the Key (page 77).

🎧 Track 2.29
10B Exercise 5

a

Presenter: Are there any questions you'd like to ask at this point? Erm, one thing you might like to know a bit more about is our subscription rates.

Audience member: Erm, yes, I was wondering about those. Is there a standard rate or does it cost more for institutional membership?

Presenter: Right, well, in fact, there is just the one standard rate, so that means for a company of your size, it actually works out very reasonable …

b

Presenter: I'm sure you have a lot of questions, which I'll be happy to answer now. Ahah! OK, this always happens, doesn't it? Everybody's got a question but nobody wants to be the first to ask. Oh, yes?

Audience member: Erm, going back to what you were saying about online payments …

c

Presenter: I think we've got about ten minutes for Q&A. So, if anybody has a question, they'd like to ask, erm … Yes, actually, I know, could I ask you to just turn to a neighbour and compare your thoughts on some of the things we've talked about this morning. And I'll take any questions in a moment. OK …

🎧 Track 2.30
10B Exercise 7

Extract 1:

Audience member: Erm, going back for a moment to what you were saying about the product life cycle.

Presenter: Eh, yes.

Audience member: You claimed that thirteen and a half percent of our market are what you called early adopters. Could you tell us how you arrived at that figure?

Presenter: Certainly. Basically, what we did is take a look at the purchasing records for the last five years …

Extract 2:

Audience member: I want to take you up on what you said about diversification being a complete waste of time.

Presenter: Yes, I know that may seem an extreme view, but I can provide you with a long list of companies in this industry who've tried a diversification strategy and failed miserably.

Audience member: Yes, I'm sure you can. But you still haven't answered my question, which is: how are we supposed to grow in such a massively over-supplied market without diversification?

Presenter: OK, well, first of all, let me say that …

Extract 3:

Audience member: I think you mentioned something about product development being a safer strategy than new market development. Could you just elaborate on that?

Presenter: Well, sure, but I don't quite see what bearing that has on today's meeting.

Audience member: OK, then. Well, let me put it another way. As you know, we already operate in several different domestic markets, but what we lack is global presence …

Extract 4:

Audience member: When you were outlining some of the ideas behind viral marketing, you said something about 'sneezers'. What exactly did you mean by that?

Presenter: Erm, well, simply that there are some customers, 'sneezers', who actually spread a company's message for it without the need for direct marketing.

Audience member: Well, OK, but, erm, one thing I'm still not clear about. Did you say that conventional marketing was obsolete? Or am I mistaken?

Presenter: No, perhaps I should just go over that again …

Extract 5:

Audience member: You told us that there is still good money to be made for the last player in a declining market. Do you have any data to support that?

Presenter: Yes, you'll find a fairly comprehensive section on this in the report in front of you. It makes for interesting reading. But being the 'last player in a declining market' as you put it is actually just one of a whole series of recommendations we're making this afternoon.

Audience member: Oh, OK, fair enough. Point taken. I see what you're saying.

Key and commentary

1A Opening and closing

2 1 Attention   2 Benefit
  3 Credibility   4 Direction

3 Attention: a, c
  Benefit: d, f
  Credibility: b, g
  Direction: e, h

4 Give them a problem or puzzle, a
  surprising fact or statistic
  Quote somebody well-known
  Show them a photograph or cartoon,
  a video, a news headline
  Tell them a joke, a story or anecdote
  Explode a popular myth
  Ask them a question, to raise their
  hand, to talk to a neighbour

5

Extract 1: The speaker opens with
a rhetorical question ('What's in a
name?') and backs that up with two
examples of companies fighting
over a name: Apple Corps v. Apple
Computers over the name 'Apple' and
Anheuser-Busch v. Budvar over the
name 'Budweiser'. In two words, the
speaker's topic, as he says himself, is
brand identity.

Extract 2: The speaker explodes the
myth that mergers don't work by
pointing out that it's only mega-
mergers between corporate giants
that so often fail. She then gives two
examples of big research-intensive
companies, Pfizer (biotech) and Cisco
(IT), taking over many innovative start-
ups highly successfully.

Extract 3: The speaker asks her
audience to raise their hand if they've
backed up their hard disc. Hardly
anybody has done it recently and
some never. The analogy between this
and going to the dentist is that it's
something we keep meaning to do but
keep putting off.

Extract 4: The speaker introduces the
topic of competitiveness by quoting
the former chairman of RCA Records,
by telling a joke about the rivalry
between Coca-Cola and Pepsi and by
asking the audience to briefly discuss
the topic with a neighbour. The quote
is probably a less risky strategy than
the joke, but the two things work well
together. And by sandwiching the joke
between the quote and the audience
task, the speaker reduces that risk.

Extract 5: The speaker lets his audience
know he understands their business by
taking time to outline the typical kind
of problems they have to face, and one
in particular – cash flow. He asks them
what it would be like to be able to
pass that problem on to someone else
and to know that it would be worth
many times the fee that person would
charge. Of course, that question is his
opportunity to introduce the answer –
the service his company offers.

7 a know   b raise   c turn
  d imagine   e said
  f misconception   g joke   h like

1B Opening and closing

2 dramatic summary 2
  famous wise words 4
  call for action 1
  heart-felt message 3

3 Probably Extract 3. It's certainly the
  one which addresses the audience
  most directly and on an emotional
  level. Extract 1 is also a direct appeal
  to the audience, but somehow lacks
  the same degree of empathy.

4 Summary: a, f, g, k
  Action: c, h, m
  Wisdom: b, i, l
  Emotion: d, e, j

5 The secret is not to make your
  summary sound like a summary.
  Don't announce it as a summary. Or,
  if you do, don't just repeat in brief
  what you've already said. Phrase the
  summary as a question, introduce
  new supporting information and try
  to build up to a powerful one-line
  close, as Quentin Willson does in his
  presentation of the E-Type.

6 *Possible answer*

Ray-Ban Wayfarers (1952–)

So, how do you sum up a pair of
sunglasses like these? I could tell you
that they are probably the bestselling
designer eyewear in history, that
they were the first sunglasses to make
use of new plastics technology and
that popular icons from James Dean
and Marilyn Monroe to Heath Ledger
and Michael Jackson were all lifelong
fans. But that would be to sell them
short. They were, are and always will
be a timeless classic and irresistibly
desirable. Wayfarers are quite simply
the coolest sunglasses in the world.

7

'The Loop' technique is where you
return to the subject you opened with
at the close of your presentation. It's
especially effective because it creates
a perfect circle and a satisfying sense
of completion. Skilful speakers often
build up audience anticipation at the
beginning of their talk and then keep
them in suspense until the end when
they finally finish their story, give the
punchline to their joke or answer the
question they posed right at the start.

2A Smooth structure

1

In a presentation, as on a journey,
you may want to 'turn off the main
road' and change the subject or even
digress for a moment. You may want to
speed up or slow down or go back to
a place you passed earlier that looked
interesting. Whenever you change
direction in a presentation, as on a car
journey, it's a good idea to indicate.
'Signpost language' helps you do that.

2

I'm going to start off by …
outlining our main goals today.
giving you a brief overview.
asking you all a question.
Let's move on to the subject of …
I'll be coming on to this later.
OK, turning for a moment to the
question of …
To return to my main point here.
Let's expand on that a little.
Going back to what I was saying
earlier.
To digress for a moment.
In closing, I'll just …
summarise the main points we've
looked at.
ask you to remember one thing.
leave you with this …

3
a Earlier we saw ... ⬅
b This leads us on to ... ➡
c As you'll recall ... ⬅
d Later we'll see ... ➡
e You'll remember ... ⬅
f So, the next question is ... ➡
g As we discussed ... ⬅
h This brings us on to ... ➡
i This goes back to ... ⬅
j By the end of this talk ... ➡

4

a Turnover for Q3 is well up, **thanks mostly to** increased sales in Russia.
(effect ➡ cause)
b Avoiding risk is a mistake, **especially** in the long term.
(point ➡ specification)
c We need to constantly reassess **so that** we don't lose our competitive lead.
(action ➡ purpose)
d A rise in the price of oil **has resulted in** reduced profitability.
(cause ➡ effect)
e Demand is down 3% in Japan, **whereas** in the rest of Asia it's tripled.
(point ➡ contrast)
f There's no market for low quality, **and what's more,** there never will be. (point ➡ addition)
g The recent flood of cheap imports **may lead to** a price war.
(cause ➡ effect)
h We need to move fast **in order to** take advantage of this opportunity.
(action ➡ purpose)
i Our share price has soared **as a result of** the merger announcement.
(effect ➡ cause)
j Now is the time to focus – **in particular** on what it is we do best.
(point ➡ specification)
k Our website's receiving more hits, **and yet** these have not converted into sales.
(point ➡ contrast)
l It's an enormous market; **plus,** it's a growing one.
(point ➡ addition)

5 *Answers top left to bottom right:*

Then I'd like to talk you through the main phases of the project.
First I'm briefly going to give you some background.
I'd like to start off by outlining our main goals today.
First of all, I'm going to give you a brief overview of the project.
Then I'd like to fill you in on some of the details.
But before we start, let me ask you a question.

Let's move on to the subject of planning.
Turning for a moment to the question of schedules.
Moving on to some of the initial problems we faced.
By the end of this talk I hope you'll have a clearer idea of the progress we've made so far.
So the next question is: how did we deal with the cultural differences?
If I could just digress for a moment here.
Just to return to my main point for a minute.
This leads us on to the question of virtual teams.
Perhaps I should just expand on that a little.
We'll be coming on to this later.
Going back to what I was saying earlier.
I'll be saying more about this later on.
This brings us on to the question of budgeting.
I'd like to take a moment to talk about logistics.
In closing, I'd just like to summarise some of the main points we've looked at.
OK, well, that brings me to the end of my presentation. Thanks very much.
In conclusion, it has, in general, been a very successful project.
OK, so we've looked at logistics. Let's finish by talking about the next phase.
Are there any questions you'd like to ask at this point?

2B Smooth structure

1 When planning your presentation, it's a good idea to switch off the computer and 'go analogue'. Forget about designing your slides at this stage and just concentrate instead on mapping out the subjects you want to cover. Post-its can work well for this. Write each topic on a separate Post-it and, when you have several, you can start moving them around to see in what order they should come. This approach also helps you to see what subjects you could drop, what's missing and where you could usefully add visuals or stories to illustrate and support your points. Then, when you're ready, switch your computer back on and 'go digital'.

A few points to remember at the planning stage:
• you know where you're going, but your audience doesn't, so make sure you signal the stages of your presentation clearly

• beware 'the curse of knowledge', where you assume your audience knows (and cares!) as much as you do; don't over-complicate things
• if there's good news to deliver, save the best till last
• if there's bad news to deliver, sandwich it between two pieces of good news
• if you're delivering information that is familiar to your audience, elicit some of the information from them, keep the presentation short and adopt an interesting creative structure
• if you're delivering information that's new to your audience, then include all the stages of thinking, allow plenty of time to fully explore the topic and stick to a conventional linear structure.

3

There are no fixed answers here. Much will depend on context, audience expectations and individual presentation style. But the following structures would work well:

a plan ▶ potential objections ▶ key benefits ▶ recommendations
b customer need ▶ main features ▶ key benefits ▶ costs
c targets ▶ results ▶ implications
d competition ▶ us ▶ future
e past ▶ present ▶ implications
f problem ▶ causes ▶ options ▶ recommendations
g idea ▶ research ▶ data ▶ key benefits
h customer need ▶ opportunity ▶ market potential ▶ costs
i need ▶ plan ▶ costs
j aims ▶ past ▶ present
k issue ▶ data ▶ decision ▶ implications
l idea ▶ aims ▶ procedure ▶ results

4 1 proverb ▶ popular myth ▶ data ▶ actual fact
2 audience task ▶ product features ▶ customer benefits ▶ comparison
3 surprising statistic ▶ threat ▶ opportunity ▶ action

5

In a well-structured presentation the key phrases and expressions the presenter uses tell you what he or she is doing at each stage of their talk – listing options, making recommendations, comparing figures, etc. This makes it much easier for an audience to follow.

6 a popular myth
   b truth
   c data
   d comparison
   e features
   f benefits
   g potential objections
   h implications
   i options
   j issues
   k pros and cons
   l projections

7 Slide 1: management, people
   Slide 2: technology, divisions, communication
   Slide 3: mandatory, forum, restructure
   Slide 4: Knowledge Management, online, intranet, workshops

3A Voice power

1

a The much-quoted statistic that what you say only accounts for 7% of your message, whilst how you sound accounts for 38% and how you look for 55%, originates in the research of Albert Mehrabian at UCLA in the 1960s. But it is a misinterpretation of his work, which concerned why people like or dislike you and not how they respond to you when you speak in public. All great speakers impress through the power of their voice. How you sound is the most direct reflection of your personality. The word 'persona' literally means 'through sound'.

b Pausing is deliberate. You hesitate when you're not sure how to continue. A good use of pausing gives both speaker and audience time to think. The audience is able to digest what it has just heard and speculate about what might be coming next. This allows them to be more involved in the presentation as silent participants and not just receivers.

c Probably the most effective place to pause is after 'effective'. Two pauses could come after 'word' and 'effective'; three after 'word', 'effective' and 'timed'; four after 'word', 'effective', 'rightly' and 'timed'. Too many pauses creates a staccato effect.

d You can overdo pauses if you make them too long – the audience might think you've forgotten what to say next. But remember that pauses always seem a lot longer to the speaker than to the listener.

If you keep eye contact with your audience, you can pause for quite a long time.

2 Version 1: Conversation
Version 2: Presentation

3 Conversation: a, d
Presentation: b, c, e, f

4 *See answers in* **6** *below.*

5 The stressed words tend to be key content words – usually nouns and main verbs. The pauses tend to come after stressed words.

6

The speaker's voice usually goes up in the middle of an utterance (indicating he hasn't finished) and down at the end to show completion.

'You know, ↑ there are a lot of myths about speaking in public. ↓ Myth number one ↑ is that what you actually say ↑ is only seven percent of the message. ↓ Thirty-eight percent is how you sound ↑ and fifty-five percent is how you look. ↓ But think about it. ↓ I mean, ↑ if that was true, ↑ you could go to a talk in Swahili ↑ and still understand ninety-three percent! ↓ Myth number two ↑ is that public speaking is most people's greatest fear ↓ – just above death. ↓ The comedian Jerry Seinfeld ↑ has a great joke about that. ↓ He says, ↑ "Come on, ↑ if it really was their greatest fear, ↑ at a funeral ↑ the person giving the eulogy ↑ would rather be in the box!" ↓'

7

Fewer pauses and stresses will make you sound quite fluent and conversational, but it will be difficult to give power and emphasis to anything you say. If you talk like this for too long, you may start to sound a bit monotonous and boring. More pauses and stresses will make you sound more enthusiastic and dynamic, but you may exhaust your audience if you overdo it. Talk like this for too long and you may start to sound over-dramatic and lacking in rapport. Try to aim for a balance of conversational and presentational styles to gain maximum impact.

8

Never try to be something you're not in a presentation. Capitalise on your strengths, making some allowance for

your audience's preferences. It's good to learn how to vary your voice, but remember that the most important thing is to be authentic.

3B Voice power

1

In the first version, the speaker *ums* and *ers* whenever she hesitates. This sounds quite distracting and makes what she is saying difficult to follow. In the second version she doesn't say any more or speak any faster, but instead of the *umming* and *erring*, she pauses. This actually makes her easier to follow and what she says easier to remember.

3

a We haven't seen a massive improvement yet. But it's a good start.

b We haven't seen a massive improvement yet. But my guess is we soon will.

c The market may be declining. But fortunately our market share isn't.

d The market may be declining. Or this could just be a temporary blip.

e We do pretty well in the States. But we don't do so well in Europe.

f We do pretty well in the States. But not as well as we could be doing.

g Turnover is up on Q3. But profits are down.

h Turnover is up on Q3. But that was a particularly bad quarter.

i It's hard to gain a foothold in India. But not impossible.

j It's hard to gain a foothold in India. But harder still to gain one in China.

k There are a couple of points I'd like to make. And both concern cash flow.

l There are a couple of points I'd like to make. And then I'll hand you over to Jan.

6

Andrew Jorgenson speaks slowly and deliberately. He uses quite long sentences, but breaks them up with frequent pauses. It's a very emotional speech and he uses a lot of imagery of death and destruction to convey his message. Jorgensen builds up from a quiet opening to a louder closing personal attack on Garfield.

'I want to share with you ↑ | some of my thoughts ↑ | concerning the vote that you're going to make ↑ | in the company that you own. ↓ || This proud company, ↑ | which has survived the death of its founder, ↑ |

numerous recessions, ↑ | one major depression, ↑ | and two world wars, ↑ || is in imminent danger of self-destructing ↓ | – on this day, ↑ | in the town of its birth. ↓ ||| There ↑ || is the instrument ↑ | of our destruction. ↓ || I want you to look at him ↑ | in all of his glory, ↑ | Larry the Liquidator, ↑ | the entrepreneur of post-industrial America, ↑ || playing God ↑ | with other people's money. ↓ ||| This man leaves nothing. ↓ || He creates nothing, ↓ | he builds nothing, ↓ | he runs nothing. ↓ '

Lawrence Garfield speaks in short staccato sentences. He uses simple words and a certain amount of sarcastic humour. He varies his voice a lot, switching from almost a whisper to louder sections. He echoes Jorgenson's death theme, but turns it around, claiming the company had destroyed itself before he arrived.

'This company is dead. ↓ || I didn't kill it. ↓ | Don't blame me. ↓ | It was dead when I got here. ↓ ||| It's too late for prayers. ↓ || For even if the prayers were answered, ↑ | and a miracle occurred, ↑ | and the yen did this, ↑ | and the dollar did that, ↑ | and the infrastructure did the other thing, ↑ || we would still be dead. ↓ | || You know why? ↑ || Fiber optics. ↓ | New technologies. ↓ || Obsolescence. ↓ | We're dead all right. ↓ | We're just not broke. ↓ || And you know the surest way to go broke? ↑ || Keep getting an increasing share ↑ | of a shrinking market. ↓ ||| I'm not your best friend. ↓ || I'm your only friend. ↓ || I don't make anything? ↑ | I'm making you money. ↓ '

4A Visual aids

1

Since the first slide is strongly visual with very little text and the second is rather dense with textual information, it's likely Walker would prefer the first. The second slide, of course, is much more typical of most business presentations.

4

The top left slide shows a fairly unimaginative use of standard presentation software graphics. The 3D pie chart is not really helpful here, the heading is too long and the actual key figure (70%) not easily legible. The colours are rather dull too. Statistically accurate, but zero impact.

The slide below it is a definite improvement. The 2D pie chart works better and the colours link up the key figure with the heading and the landmass of India on the globe. A larger font size also helps, although the figure in green doesn't stand out very well from the green background. And, in a way, the three main elements in the slide force the audience to work out the connection between them when they should be listening to the speaker.

The top right slide has plenty of impact. The key figure stands out well and, as its connection with the photo is not immediately clear, it will be necessary for the audience to listen to the speaker to find out what it is. A very good example of collaborating with, rather than competing with, your visual aids. The photo itself is slightly humorous and illustrates well some of the joys and frustrations of working with family. A more serious photo could be substituted if felt more appropriate. A black background and white font might draw the two elements in the slide closer together.

The bottom right slide is very dark and atmospheric, but perhaps a little stereotypical. The image, however, says nothing about families. Perhaps the worst aspect of the slide is that it conveys all the information the speaker has to give, so that there is no actual need for them to speak! A pretty but fairly pointless visual aid.

5

'Career suislide' seems to refer to all the things about your slides that could kill your career – or, at least, the presentation you're giving! These would include textual overload, illegibility, lack of or irrelevant visuals, unhelpful, confusing or over-complicated graphics, poor layout or choice of colours and general ugliness!

6

a He took it out of an ordinary office envelope and showed it to the audience.

b He saw a brain researcher take an actual human brain on stage!

c He team-presented the system on stage with two holographic co-presenters.

d Jobs used the small inner pocket you find on every pair of jeans as if it had been specifically designed to carry the iPod Nano.

7

Even if you have no actual product you can use as a prop, this doesn't stop you using real objects to liven up your presentation. In some cultures, and in the creative industries in general, presenters often use a whole array of toys, hats, noise-makers and sports equipment to make their point memorable. But more conservative presenters can still make use of simple props to illustrate their message: a set of scales to illustrate balance, jigsaw pieces to illustrate teamwork, a magnifying glass to illustrate analysis, etc. The secret always is to use props with a sense of humour – and they can be a good source of humour. If used too seriously they can seem clichéd and a bit silly.

8

The general rule here is 'less is more'. The designer has, in most cases, significantly reduced the amount of data to give what's left more impact. Where this has not been possible, they have used the animation function to display the text in stages as they speak.

The designer has also resisted the temptation to tell the whole story on the slide and leave the presenter with nothing to say.

More attention has been paid to the aesthetics of the slide to draw the audience's attention. We live in an age which is very visually sophisticated, so slides must look both professionally and attractively designed.

4B Visual aids

4

The 666 Rule

The 666 Rule basically states that you should never have more than six words per bullet point, no more than six bullets per slide and no more than six bullet-point slides in a row. This is supposed to reduce the amount of textual information and make your slides easier to read. But, if you think about it, you don't really want your audience to be reading – you want them to be listening! And the 666 Rule can actually mean your audience has to get through 216 words! What are you supposed to be doing while they do that? Because if you speak, they certainly won't be listening! One solution to this problem is to display the bullets one at a time, always making sure to *tell* before you *show*.

The 10–20–30 Rule

The venture capitalist Guy Kawasaki has a very neat rule about using visuals. He calls it the 10–20–30 Rule. Ten is the number of slides you should have – just ten. And 20 is the number of minutes you should speak for. Of course, Guy's job is listening to people pitching to him for venture capital, so if you can't say it in 20 minutes in ten slides, you probably don't have much of a venture! But the best bit of the rule is the 30. Guy says don't use fonts smaller than 30 point because older people, the ones with the money, can't read them! He says find out who the oldest person in your audience is, divide their age by two and that is your optimal font size. So, as Guy puts it, 'Unless you are presenting to 16-year-olds, don't use the eight point font!'

5

Option 1

Strong colours reflect the title – golden rules.
Larger font size increases legibility.
Maximum six words per bullet – it's your job to say more about each of these.
All bullets begin with an imperative verb – this adds consistency and power.

Option 2

5 GOLDEN RULES
▶ Intros
▶ Apologies
▶ Details
▶ Stories
▶ Conversation

Strong colours again reflect the title – golden rules.

Much larger font size for legibility and impact – five is a good number to emphasise.
Single-word bullets – very punchy; but still enough to help you remember what to say. The advantage of having just single words is that they don't make much sense on their own, so the audience has to listen to you for an explanation of their significance.
All bullets are nouns, however, which are highly memorable.

Option 3

An image of five gold bars replaces the title, leaving you free to call these the five golden rules.
Embossing the font adds three-dimensional depth.

6

a 85% = percentage of American households in which women are the chief decision-makers in the purchase of all consumer goods
b 8/10 = the number of times it's the woman in those households who makes the final decision
c 75% = percentage of real-estate decisions made by women
d 10% = the amount by which women spend more online than men
e $70m = the amount by which women spent more online than men on the biggest day for web sales this year
f ¾ = the proportion of annual revenue companies lose by not marketing directly to women

7

a	look	i	background
b	axis	j	know
c	see	k	put
d	take	l	figures
e	notice	m	speak
f	point	n	suggest
g	attention	o	might
h	talk	p	question
		q	mean
		r	implications

8 *Suggested answers*

Note that it's not possible to add an adverb to all the expressions.

As you can *clearly* see …, These figures *clearly* show …, *Clearly*, the figures speak for themselves …
You'll *immediately* notice …
These figures *presumably* show …, These figures *presumably* suggest …
These figures *obviously* show …, *Obviously*, the figures speak for themselves, *Obviously*, the real question is …
I'd *particularly* like to draw your attention to …
Let's *briefly* take a closer look, To *briefly* give you the background to that, So, *briefly*, what does this mean in terms of …?, Now, *briefly*, what are the implications of this?
Frankly, the figures speak for themselves
Let's *just* take a closer look, *Just* to give you the background to that, I should *just* point out …, Now, let's *just* put that into perspective, I'd *just* like to draw your attention to …, Let me *just* talk you through …

5A Facts and figures

1

Data-dumping is a common problem, particularly in technical presentations, where the speaker is anxious to prove to their audience that they have covered all the angles and know their subject in detail. But, in fact, the best way to demonstrate your expertise is to have all the necessary data at your fingertips and, as Tom Peters recommends, only show a very small portion of it to your audience in your slides. This allows you, when your audience asks for more detail or further information, to display your command of the subject by quoting supporting figures – apparently off the top of your head. In reality, of course, you've carefully memorised all the key figures and have a copy of the rest close at hand.

2

As the extracts show, certain cultures are mistrustful of presentations that lack factual depth. Cultures as diverse as Belgium, Canada, the Czech Republic, Denmark, Finland, Germany, Israel, Korea, the Netherlands, Norway, Slovakia, Sweden and Switzerland fall into this category. Other cultures, notably Arab countries, Brazil, Britain, France, Greece, Hungary, India, Ireland, Italy, Mexico, Romania, Russia, Spain, Turkey and the USA, will tend to be more influenced by style than content, at least in the presentation itself. 'Style' may take many forms, however. For the British, Irish or Americans it will probably involve humour. For the Arabs, Greeks, Hungarians or Indians it's more likely to be a matter of eloquence. Latins will probably be looking for personal charm and charisma. Chinese and Japanese may not be especially impressed by either style or content. Anything stylish about your performance may come across as arrogant and flashy and clash with their preference for calmness and humility. And most of your facts and figures will probably be considered only of short-term interest, when their concern is mainly for the long-term future.

3

A 'slideument', as Reynolds explains, is neither a good slide nor a good handout. It contains too much information to be visually effective as a slide and not enough to give sufficient background as a handout. His suggestion that you make your slides simple and memorable and your handouts detailed and comprehensive is one good solution to this problem. Unfortunately, it is common practice in many companies (for example, in Germany) for employers to request a copy of the presenter's PowerPoint slides to email to the audience as handouts after the talk. And some conference committees expect speakers to email their slides in advance as part of their presentation proposal. Where bosses and conference organisers cannot be flexible, one solution is to have two slides for each of the key parts of your presentation – a strikingly designed overview or 'snapshot' of the most important data and a textually denser, fully contextualised slide to satisfy the data-hungry. Obviously, you would then delete the 'snapshot' slides from your set of handouts. Another option is to use the 'custom animation' function

on your PowerPoint slides to transition from the full picture to the edited highlights or vice versa.

4

There are clearly different degrees of simplification possible here. But, since the audience consists mostly of Polish women, the photographic visual is probably quite appropriate as it is. Poland, in second place in the chart, must obviously be retained (and highlighted in some way) along with Italy in the number one slot. For contrast, one or two countries should be selected from the middle and near-bottom of the chart (say, France and Germany), together with Norway, at the lower extreme. Headings and layout could also be made simpler and more memorable, so that the final slide might look something like the one below.

Men's extra leisure time (mins/day)

Italy
Poland
France
Germany
Norway

Note that this slide not only has more impact but requires the presenter to explain its significance rather than just hover in the background or state the obvious. If the audience asks, for example, where the USA ranks on the chart, the presenter can quote the relevant figures from their notes.

5 *Note that the recorded version is British rather than American English.*
a fourteen thousand, six hundred and forty
b thirty-three point three three
c nineteen ninety-nine
d twenty ten *or* two thousand and ten
e sixty dollars and ten cents
f eight point oh oh one percent
g a hundred and three million *or* a hundred and three metres (depending on the context)
h six point one billion

i half a percent (percentage point)
j (a) quarter of a percent (percentage point)
k three quarters (*AmE* sometimes three fourths)
l five eighths
m a third
n seventy-five degrees
o up two points
p (a ratio of) nine to one
q a thousand ccs (cubic centimetres)
r eighteen percent per annum
s one point three dollars to the euro
t two thousand revs (revolutions) per minute
u five and a half (five point five) square metres
v Q three (third quarter)

7

a In Q4 we saw an **almost 20%** increase in revenues.
b We've managed to bring down costs by **nearly 25%**.
c We currently have **around 100** branches in **over 200** countries.
d We've made a substantial investment of **just short of $½ bn**.
e **Just over three-quarters** of the respondents in our survey actually expressed no preference.
f The basic model comes in **more than 50** different versions.
g Turnover this year was **well in excess of €100 m**.
h The project will be completed in **approximately 2 months**.

8

a – g   b – e   c – h   d – f

5B Facts and figures

1

There's certainly a big difference between presenting to 'numbers people' (engineers, technicians, IT support, R&D, production, finance and accounting) and 'people people' (marketing and sales, HR), although nobody wants to be overloaded with endless data! The secret with numbers people is not to exaggerate or sensationalise any of the figures. Let the figures speak for themselves and do nothing to distract attention away from them. Keep things elegant and simple. With people people it's OK to put a slightly positive spin on things and to cut down the amount of interesting but non-essential information. But any audience will usually welcome a bit of celebration of positive information, so it's generally acceptable to 'dress up' the good news a little.

3 *Suggested answers*

↑
soar
skyrocket
take off
boom
shoot up
jump
leap

↗
go up
rise
increase
climb

↓
crash
plunge
plummet
slump
nosedive

↘
go down
fall
decrease
dip
drop
slip
slide

⋰→
stabilise
flatten out
even out

⋱→
bottom out

⋰→
top out

→
remain constant
remain
unchanged
hold steady

⌣↗
recover
pick up
bounce back
rally

∿
fluctuate
have / experience
a few ups and
downs

◠○
peak / reach a
peak
reach a high / an
all-time high

◡○
reach a low / an
all-time low

Nouns: a(n) boom, jump, leap, rise, increase, climb, crash, plunge, slump, nosedive, fall, decrease, dip, drop, slip, slide, stabilisation, recovery, bounce, rally, fluctuation, peak, high, low

---

4

Scale	Significance	Speed
BIG OR SMALL CHANGE?	**GOOD OR BAD CHANGE?**	**FAST OR SLOW CHANGE?**
++ massive enormous huge tremendous* dramatic*	**++** tremendous* fantastic	**++** sharp sudden alarming* dramatic*
+ marked substantial significant considerable	**+** encouraging	**+** rapid
– moderate	**–** disappointing	**–** steady
– – slight modest marginal	**– –** disastrous alarming*	**– –** gradual

* a modifier which can fulfil more than one function (simultaneously)

5 *Suggested answers*

D is marginally higher than E.
A is (just) as high as C.
B is by far the highest.
E is almost as high as D.
E is not quite as high as D.
A and C are nowhere near as high as B.
D and E are more or less the same.
D is considerably higher than A and C.
A and C are equally high.

6

– b f a c g e d +

7

An inc**reasing** share of a shr**inking** market.

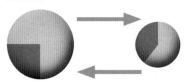

A dec**lining** share of an exp**anding** market.

THE MARKET

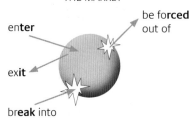

enter
be fo**rced** out of
ex**it**
br**eak** into

The market is
b**oom**ing   ++   flat   –
st**ead**y   +   de**pressed** – –

8

The ad had an immediate impact. In January our CT rate went up **by** 2½% **from** just ½% **to** 3% – an amazing six-fold increase!

Then in February we saw a drop **of** 1¾ **to** just 1¼%. But that's still well **above** average.

In March the figure fluctuated **between** a high **of** 2 and a low **of** 1%.

Finally, in April it hovered **around** 1½% to finish up **at** a little **over** that by the end of the campaign. All in all, an excellent response!

Note: People often just want to give a general overview of trends the audience can already clearly see in the visual. To do this, they may simply talk about 'the trend generally being up', 'an overall downward trend' or 'a few ups and downs'.

6A Body language

1

a For most of us, being in front of an audience is not natural, so acting natural involves imagining you're speaking to just a few friends or colleagues and adopting the same easy-going conversational tone you'd use with them. Of course, that only works if you're quite a lively and expressive conversationalist to begin with. If you're too relaxed and low-key in front of a large audience, you may lose their attention. That's why you need to make your voice just a little bit louder, your movements just a little bit more deliberate and your gestures just a little bit more expansive than usual.

b As long as you don't try to compete with your visual aids, you'll always be the audience's centre of attention. And that's what you should be. So come out from behind that podium or PowerPoint projector and let them see you!

c If the messages you're sending with your words and your body are synchronised, you'll be doubly effective. But if your words are saying one thing and your body another, people will pay more attention to your body and how you move. That's human nature. And it's why it's so easy to distract or confuse your audience with inappropriate gestures. If you repeatedly nod your head or scratch your nose, that's what they'll be fixed on!

2

a Younger audiences appreciate a more physical dynamic presenter; older audiences a calmer, more relaxed one.

b Your body language should flow naturally from what you are saying, not the other way around or you'll seem unnatural.

c He says a smile works in all cultures.

d In private conversation Arabs like to sit close together. In public speaking they compensate for the distance with expressive body language and raised voices.

3

a M – Men move around the room more.

b W – Women hold eye contact four times longer.

c W – Women gesture towards themselves.

d M – Men gesture away from themselves.

e M – Men point and wave their arms more.

f W – Women smile and nod while listening.

g M – Men tilt the head and frown while listening.

h M – Men keep their bodies fairly rigid.

4

If you are a woman presenting to a mostly male audience (especially a senior one), you might want to think about 'commanding your space' a little more by moving around the room, smiling just a little less and gesturing outwards. All these behaviours (rightly or wrongly) are associated with confidence and tend to be more typical of men. Too much smiling and nodding, in particular, can make it look like you're too anxious to please.

If you are a man presenting to a mostly female audience, you might want to wander around a bit less, but loosen up your posture a little more. To avoid coming across as arrogant or superior, try to avoid frowning when concentrating on what someone is saying to you. Remember to smile and look people directly in the eye for a second or two longer than you normally would. All these behaviours (again, rightly or wrongly) are associated with being open to and interested in your audience and tend to be more typical of women.

5

1 e 2 c 3 f 4 a 5 d 6 b

Certain gestures are famously rude in some cultures – for example, the 'OK' sign with the tip of the thumb and index finger touching is offensive in Brazil. Pointing the index and middle finger upwards with your palm inward is a rude, if now rather old-fashioned, gesture in Britain. The thumbs-up sign can also be risky in some countries. Also be careful not to punch the palm of your other hand, point directly at people or display an open palm with the fingers separated … the list goes on and on.

But there's no need to be paranoid! In general, the lively use of gesture will make your presentation much more effective than stiff immobility, so don't be inhibited. Be yourself. The audience knows you are foreign and are more likely to be amused by a couple of inappropriate gestures than offended by them. It's much more important to eliminate any distracting habits you repeatedly display – for instance, using the same gesture over and over again to emphasise points.

6B Body language

2

The qualities here are demonstrated by very different gestures, postures and movements. You can combine them, of course, but it's difficult to be all things to all people. You need to decide what kind of image you want to project and work on that. Openness, honesty and approachability are reflected in open gestures, smiling and good eye contact. Enthusiasm and energy are chiefly shown in mobility and talking with the hands more. Leadership and confidence come through a more controlled use of movement with nothing hurried and a firm standing position. For charisma, the X Factor, there is no magic recipe, except to look as though you're enjoying the moment and would rather be giving this presentation right here right now to this audience than doing anything else.

3

Authority: wait, use subtle gestures, talk slowly, look slightly above the audience, stand still, imagine your presence fills the room, say less, talk low

Rapport: maintain lots of eye contact, ask lots of questions, use humour, listen, imagine you're talking to a small group of friends, get excited

7

a After the presenter's face, their hands are the thing the audience will notice the most, especially if they are used a lot. It's OK to gesture a lot as long as you vary your gestures. They only become distracting if they are habitual and repeated.

b Folding your arms keeps your hands still, but restricts your ability to express yourself. More importantly, it creates a barrier between you and your audience. Standing behind a podium creates a similar barrier and is also very restricting. The solution to 'the podium trap' is to insist on having a radio microphone and the freedom to move around if you want to.

c Fiddling with objects makes a 'hands problem' worse. Clicking pens, adjusting ties, playing with jewellery, shirt cuffs or loose change in your pockets are all extremely distracting. So empty your pockets, don't wear dangly jewellery, put pens away and leave items of clothing alone!

d People who are nervous often move around a lot and wave their hands about, so people who move around too much may appear nervous, even if they're not. Being relaxed is good; being over-relaxed makes you look as if you don't really care. Hands on hips or in pockets can give this impression. So try to make sure you stand still between movements and appear alert to your audience.

9

Picture a shows the 'penguin position' with the back stiff and arms limp at your sides. Not only does this lower your own energy levels and make you look a bit uncomfortable speaking in public but it also drains energy from the audience, who take their lead from you. Your arms are not passengers! Make them do some of the work.

Picture b shows what communications coach Tim Koegel calls the 'T. Rex'. Here the presenter moves quickly around the room with their hands held up high by their face and a fixed grin. The impression is one of over-anxiousness to please and false cheerfulness.

Picture c illustrates the so-called 'fig-leaf position'. Here the presenter clasps their hands in front of them like a frightened rabbit. The idea is that this stops you waving your arms about and looks calm and professional. In fact, it usually makes you look over-formal and prevents you from expressing yourself with your hands. It can also look a bit defensive. Remember, you're facing an audience not facing a free kick in a football match!

The position in picture d is sometimes called 'parade rest'. It involves folding your hands behind your back as soldiers do in the army. At best, this looks a bit confrontational. At worst it can look as if you're hiding something from the audience!

Picture e shows the 'caged tiger'. This is where the presenter paces up and down in front of their audience. Such behaviour is usually the result of nerves as the speaker tries to use up excess energy. If punctuated with periods of standing still, it can sometimes be quite dynamic. If continuous, it can be very tiring for both speaker and audience!

7A Rapport building

1

a Creating an impression of openness to your audience has a lot to do with your body language. If you appear relaxed and comfortable in front of them, they'll relax and be comfortable too. Audiences take their lead from you. If *you* appear nervous and self-conscious, you'll make *them* tense as well. If, on the other hand, you come across as over-confident, you may antagonise them into resisting your message. Good eye contact is essential. Talk *to* them, not *at* them! Smile from time to time. Project your voice a little more than usual, but not so much that it sounds as if you're lecturing. Try to make your presentation sound more like a conversation. If you're presenting to a roomful of strangers, it may help to imagine you're addressing a group of colleagues or friends. After all, that's what you hope they'll be by the end of your talk.

b To communicate is to connect. The word 'communication' comes from related Latin words meaning 'to have something in common', 'to share a mutual objective', 'to strengthen connections'. To connect with an audience, they need to like you. And to like you, they need to like something in you that is like something they like in themselves. The more you 'talk their language' and show them that you've had many of the same thoughts and experiences they have, the more you'll connect. A good piece of advice if you're presenting at a conference is to talk to members of your audience as they arrive, find out a few names, ask them about their jobs and what brings them to the event. This will help you to relax and overcome any last-minute nerves. And when you begin your presentation it will be more like talking to people you know than to total strangers. Also, if you can refer to at least one or two people by name as you're speaking, ask them a simple question or two, it really helps to build rapport with the whole audience.

c In a conversation people are motivated to listen by the fact that they may have to speak next. In a presentation the audience knows it may not be able to speak until the end – and needn't speak at all. Down goes motivation to listen! If, as a presenter, you give your audience small opportunities to participate as you speak (perhaps by directly asking them questions or getting them to do things), you turn a presentation into more of a conversation and audience motivation goes up. But make sure you stop and listen if they do respond to you. You may be able to use something they say to connect to what you were about to say next or relate what you say next back to something they said earlier. Either way, you've shown you were listening! And don't worry about the audience distracting you from your plan. You don't need to be word-perfect. In fact, most audiences prefer a speech that sounds as if it's at least partly spontaneous to one which is totally rehearsed.

d If your presentation topic matters to *you*, it will matter to your audience. Correction: if your topic *appears* to matter to you, it will matter to them. It's vital that you convey a real sense of enthusiasm for your subject and have some fun with it as you speak. Just *being* interested in your theme is not enough. When an audience attends your presentation, they are giving you permission to have a good time. Having a good time doesn't mean joking around or being manically energetic. But it does usually mean increasing your energy level to fill the room. Enthusiasm is infectious and so is the lack of it. Remember the last time you watched a TV documentary about a subject you were not especially interested in to begin with, but the presenter brought it so much to life, you watched it right through till the end? That's the kind of passion you want to create.

2

a Now, we know this is something that affects each and every one of us.
b I think we'd all agree that in the long term this is in our best interests.
c We need to be asking ourselves: what are we trying to achieve?
d So do we or don't we take up the challenge? The choice is ours.
e We've got three amazing new products we want to share with you today. So let's get started!

3 a is it?   d haven't we?
   b will we?   e didn't I?
   c can we?   f don't you?

4 a Shouldn't we …?
   b Offshoring – isn't this …?
   c Isn't it …?
   d Haven't we …?
   e Isn't there …?
   f Aren't we …?

5 a – m   e – i
   b – k   f – j
   c – h   g – l
   d – n

6 *Involvement expressions:*

If you're anything like me, …
I don't know about you, but …
When was the last time you …?
Raise your hand if …
I think that's something we can all relate to.
So, what if I was to say to you …?
You'd think I was crazy, right?
Let me ask you a question.
How many of you …?
If, like me, you find …
But let me share some statistics with you.
Did you know that …?
And would it surprise you to learn that …?
Now, I know what you're thinking.
But, you see, that's where you'd be wrong.
And you don't need me to tell you …

7B Rapport building

1

a Being funny will help you to entertain an audience – providing they like your sense of humour! But being fun is more inclusive and a lot less risky. Audiences can participate in the fun and even occasionally take the lead. They are not just on the receiving end. As Doni Tamblyn has pointed out, when you're funny, it makes an audience feel good about you; when you're fun, it makes them feel good about themselves. Ideally, you want them to feel both. A presentation should be a shared experience.

Another source of fun, if you don't feel you want to try and be funny yourself, is to use humorous quotes instead. You can find thousands of these on the Internet. And you can simply show them in a slide or actually deliver them yourself. If they're not well known, you could even try pretending they're your own! You wouldn't be the first person to do that.

b One good way of creating opportunities for laughter to naturally emerge is to constantly be listening and talking to your audience. Often they will initiate the humour. Some audiences are more reluctant to participate than others. But, if you've succeeded in relaxing them and getting them to trust you, they are much more likely to be responsive and share their humour with you.

Of course, fun doesn't necessarily have to involve humour. Asking your audience to take part in a short lively activity can also generate laughter. And if you can laugh at yourself when things go wrong – your radio mike falls off, your video link freezes – you can save a lot of embarrassment: 'My radio mike just committed suicide', 'Can we turn the central heating up? My video link's frozen'.

2 *Pros:*

• humorous stories are memorable and, if relevant, help you get your message across more effectively

• laughter raises energy levels, a good thing in any talk, but especially a long one

• humour is something both speaker and audience can share, so you build rapport through laughter

• it gives your audience a breathing space between different parts of your presentation and can even help you to phase your talk

• it reduces stress; when the audience laughs everyone can relax, you included

Cons:

• humour can be distracting, especially if it has no connection with what you're talking about

• it can confuse an audience whose English is not so good

• it can be embarrassing if it looks as if you're expecting a laugh and you don't get one – it takes a while to recover from a failed joke*

• in cultures very different from your own it can be easy to unintentionally give offence by using the wrong kind of humour**

* The secret of recovering from a joke that nobody noticed is simply to move on; if they did notice, but didn't laugh, then always admit the failure somehow ('My husband gave me that joke. Thanks, honey.').
** Verbal humour and wordplay are the most 'easily lost in translation', but other simpler kinds of physical or visual humour may still work well.

4

There is some overlap between some of the intelligence types. Here are the suggested answers with possible alternatives in brackets.

1 Visual: a, e, n, v, x
2 Auditory: b, r (p)
3 Logical: d, i, p, t
4 Physical/spatial: f, h, l, o, u, w, y
5 Interpersonal: j, m, s
6 Intrapersonal: c, g, k, q (f, o)

5

Extract 1: physical/spatial / visual / interpersonal
Extract 2: visual / logical / intrapersonal
Extract 3: auditory / intrapersonal
Extract 4: visual / physical/spatial / interpersonal
Extract 5: visual / logical
Extract 6: visual / auditory / interpersonal
Extract 7: visual / physical/spatial / interpersonal
Extract 8: visual / physical/spatial / interpersonal

Note that handouts, cards and objects combine the visual with the more physical. Some people need to see things on a handout they can hold in front of them rather than on a screen in the distance. Getting audience members to work in pairs or groups obviously encourages interpersonal processing of information, whilst getting them occasionally to work alone encourages inner reflection. Remember that most presentations consist of a lot of talking, so the auditory channel is already open most of the time. Remember also that we live in a highly (tele)visual age, so whatever intelligences you address, it's generally good to include the visual in there somewhere.

8A Impact techniques

1

Examples of repetition from Tracy Goodwin's comments include: complete sentences ('I want to talk a minute about repetition'); adverbs ('very, very important'); semi-fixed expressions ('You … the speech'); sound repetition ('repeat and restate the important points' /r/, /p/ and /t/).

An example of restatement is the rephrasing of 'very, very important in any speech that you do two things – repetition, restatement' as: 'You have to repeat and restate the important points.'

2

a matter ▶ question
b absolute ▶ total
c objectives ▶ goals
d information ▶ data
e drop ▶ decline
f nothing ▶ zero

3 a up   f never
  b always   g nobody
  c time   h long
  d why   i today
  e really

4 a nowhere   d nothing
  b no one   e anything
  c everyone   f everything

6

The repeated sounds are shown in phonemic transcript; learners only need to highlight the letters in the words and identify the sounds orally.

Holiday Inn: /p/ and /iː/
Royal Dutch Shell: /ʃ/
Microsoft: /w/ and /t/
Carlsberg: /b/ and /ə/
United Airlines: /f/ and /aɪ/
Jaguar: /d/ and /t/
Philips: /s/ and /ɪ/
Fila: /f/, /ʃ/, /ə/ and /b/

7

a advertised ▶ promoted
b significant ▶ major
c easy ▶ simple
d company ▶ firm
e group ▶ team
f option ▶ choice
g under ▶ bust / broke / bankrupt

8

There'll always … always be a market for quality. And quality is what I want to talk to you about today. So what do I know about quality? I know three things. I know it's better. I know it costs more. And, crucially, I know customers actually want it to cost more. Because it's not about your products; it's about how people perceive your products. As Stella Artois's brilliant beer ad used to put it: 'Reassuringly expensive'. I know no better definition of quality.

8B Impact techniques

1

a *Repetition of words and sounds*
 Words
 any(thing / one)
 techniques
 speakers / speak
 Sounds
 successful speakers (/s/)
 inspire, persuade (/s/, /p/)
 enthuse their audiences (/z/)
 rhetorical techniques (/t/)
 alive and well (/l/)
 speakers speak (/s/, /p/, /k/)
b *Rhetorical questions*
 Is there anything you can do to get your message across with greater impact? Are there any techniques that all successful speakers use to inspire, persuade and enthuse their audiences? And, if so, can anyone learn to use them? (The three opening sentences are all rhetorical questions.)
c *Groups of three*
 Is there anything you can do to get your message across with greater impact? Are there any techniques that all successful speakers use to **inspire, persuade and enthuse** their audiences? And, if so, can anyone learn to use them? (A group of three within a group of three.)

2

Rhetorical questions can be a powerful presentation tool because they seem to address the members of the audience directly and ask them to think about the question, even if they are not supposed to actually answer it. They make the speaker's monologue sound more like a dialogue (always a good thing) and encourage involvement in the issue and anticipation of the answer, which, if it is not obvious, the speaker usually goes on to give. Rhetorical questions are one very effective way of making a presentation more conversational, thereby building rapport.

3

a So, what's the main challenge we face? The main challenge is piracy.
b So, what's the answer? The answer is viral marketing.
c So, what's the problem? The problem is converting leads into sales.
d So, where are the best opportunities? The best opportunities are in China.
e So, what's my point? My point is that big-budget advertising simply doesn't work.
f So, what's the plan? The plan is to give our project teams more autonomy.

4

a Now what can we do about that?
b But what do I mean by that?
c Now how can we improve that?
d But didn't we know that already?
e So what are the alternatives?
f But what will this mean in practice?

5

a how + do
b what + waiting
c where + did
d what + do
e how much + wasted
f why + selling
g where + go
h what + talking
i how soon + expect

7 a – e   b – f   c – d

8 a – e – c   b – f – a   c – d – b

8C Impact techniques

1

a This **time next** year, we'll be **number one**.
b It's a **matter** of **doing** the **right things**.
c I'm **asking you** not to **say no**.
d I'm **saying** it's **our only option**.
e I **say leap**, **then look**.
f **Today**, it has **become** a **reality**.
g … **someone else will**.
h … but we **can still** be the **best**.

3

a huge, enormous, immense
b transformed, revolutionised
c brand-new, innovative, revolutionary, breakthrough
d destroyed, wiped out, outclassed, defeated, slaughtered

e striking, fabulous, gorgeous, eye-catching, breath-taking
f slashed
g great, superb, terrific, fantastic
h soared, taken off, (sky)rocketed, gone through the roof

4

a We've done **exceptionally** well this year – **even** better than last year, in fact.
b If we **truly** believe in this company, we need to be **one hundred percent** committed to its success.
c It's done **dramatically** better than we expected in **such** a short space of time.
d It's **just so** encouraging to see people **really** working together as a team.
e We now **totally** dominate the sector, even though it's **so highly** competitive.
f We've invested **heavily / heavily** invested in R&D and I'm **absolutely** delighted to say that that investment has paid off **a hundredfold**.
g Every unit has performed **superlatively** well and I **genuinely** believe this is **just** the beginning of a **tremendously** exciting period for this company.

5

1 Business is a sport
 win back market share, play as a team, level the playing field, be in a different league
2 Business is a race
 outpace our competitors, fall behind, be overtaken, catch up with the market leaders
3 Business is war
 wipe out the competition, join forces, come under attack, rethink our strategy, reinforce our position, bring out the big guns, hit the ground running
4 Business is a construction site
 build a firm foundation for future business, build a reputation, reconstruct our image, get in on the ground floor
5 Business is nature
 grow our business, start to see the fruits of our efforts, get to the root of the problem, cultivate relationships

6

a For the last three years we've enjoyed **spectacular** success.
b It's been a really **outstanding** performance all round.
c First indications are the situation could be **catastrophic**.

d This really is a **revolutionary** idea.

e We're talking about **cutting-edge** technology.

f The new designs are absolutely **stunning**.

g It's **enormously** difficult to make long-term predictions.

h Customer response has been **truly** remarkable.

i The latest figures are **extremely** encouraging.

j The whole campaign has been **phenomenally** successful.

k Even though there's a risk, it's crucial to our success.

l Other people say it can't be done, but I say we're the ones to do it.

m Maybe we can't be number one in the world, but we can in Asia.

n We need to **build bridges between** departments.

o We have to **close the gap on** the competition.

p We can't just **plough more money into** R&D.

8D Impact techniques

1

An important similarity between acting and presenting is that both involve a strong element of performance. The ability to use your voice, gestures and posture effectively is just as important in both. Some speakers have natural presence; others have to learn how to perform in a way that suggests they have presence.

If performance is what you do, presence is what you are. Gaps in your presence can be worked on as elements of your performance:

Presence	Performance
You're calm	Slow down, breathe evenly, smile
You're confident	Project and lower your voice, don't fidget
You're entertaining	Be playful, tell stories, let humour emerge
You're provocative	Challenge orthodoxy, take calculated risks
You're charismatic	Look as if you're enjoying yourself, laugh
You have rapport	Converse with and involve your audience

If you feel you lack, but would like to develop, the characteristics on the left, you can begin by starting to do more of the things on the right. At first, this may feel a little unnatural, but eventually your performance will become second nature. Performance will become presence. Until then, fake it till you make it!

Alternatively, you can stop worrying about the characteristics you don't have and concentrate on improving the ones you do!

The most important difference between acting and presenting is that an actor is trying to persuade you they are someone else. If they forget their lines, hesitate or say things wrong, they lose credibility. A presenter is only trying to be themselves, to be authentic in front of an audience. Interestingly, presenters gain credibility when they hesitate, have to think, change direction, improvise. We then believe they are talking to us spontaneously and not simply reciting a rehearsed speech.

'Over-presenting', which is like over-acting, is what happens when the presenter comes across as too rehearsed and too focused on themselves and their performance. Sometimes, people who belong to public speaking clubs and societies are trained to speak in this way. It might work in certain cultures. But generally, the result is that you look like a third-rate actor or stand-up comedian. Unless you could be a first-rate actor or stand-up comedian, don't do this! Once you know your material, focus on your audience at all times, not on what you are doing. The more your monologue sounds like a dialogue, the more authentic you'll appear. And authenticity is the key.

2

Sound repetition highlighted.

Dan Futterman in *Shooting Fish*

Mr Greenaway, do you know why you're here? [rhetorical question] You're here [word repetition] to see technology at its most advanced. You're here [word repetition] to buy a seventh-generation computer. A computer [word repetition] you can talk to. A computer [word repetition] that'll talk to you. [word repetition] This is Johnson. It's the first computer [word repetition] to be truly free of a keyboard. Mr Greenaway, [word repetition] nobody likes to type. Everybody likes to talk. [word repetition, contrast] Do you like to talk? [word repetition, rhetorical question] I like to talk. [word repetition] Johnson here [word repetition] doesn't just understand three thousand words, not just six thousand words [word repetition] – the common everyday vocabulary of you or me – Johnson [word repetition] understands eighty thousand and twenty-four words. [word repetition, contrast, group of three]

Michael Douglas in *Wall Street*

I am not a destroyer of companies. I am a liberator of them. [contrast] The point is, ladies and gentlemen, that greed, for lack of a better word, is good. Greed [word repetition] is right. Greed works. [word repetition, group of three] Greed [word repetition] clarifies, cuts through and captures [group of three] the essence of the evolutionary spirit. Greed [word repetition] in all of its forms. Greed [word repetition] for life, for money, for love, [group of three] knowledge [plus one] has marked the upward surge of mankind and greed [word repetition], you mark my words, will not only save Teldar Paper, but that other malfunctioning corporation called the USA. [contrast]

Aaron Eckhart in *Thank You for Smoking*

In 1910 the US was producing 10 billion cigarettes a year. By 1930 we were up to 123 billion. [contrast] What happened in between? [rhetorical question] Three things: a world war, dieting and movies. [group of three] 1927: talking pictures are born. Suddenly, directors need to give their actors something to do while they're talking. Cary Grant, Carole Lombard are lighting up; Bette Davis: a chimney. [group of three] And Bogart: remember the first picture with him and Lauren Bacall? [rhetorical question] She says 'Anyone got a match?' And Bogey throws the matches at her and she catches them – greatest romance of the century. How'd it start? [rhetorical question] Lighting a cigarette. These days when someone smokes in the movies, they're either a psychopath or a European. [contrast] The message Hollywood needs to send out is: smoking is cool. Most of the actors smoke already. [word repetition] If they start doing it on screen, we can put the sex back into cigarettes.

6

a Carly Fiorina uses a great deal of repetition in her presentations. She particularly likes using a technique the ancient Greeks called 'anaphora' – starting consecutive sentences or clauses with identical or nearly identical words and phrases:

FedEx **was told** *they'd never make an overnight delivery service work. Amazon* **was told** *they'd never make online retailing work. BMW's Formula One team* **was told** *they'd never make a car that rivals Ferrari.*
In every single case, *they proved the skeptics wrong. And* **in every single case**, *HP was there.*
But in these uncertain times, it is **our capacity to** *look ahead,* **our capacity to** *build a better future,* **our capacity to** *develop practical solutions that make our work all the more essential.*

Note also the use of groups of three in two of the examples above. The effect of using repetition in a presentation is both to make sure the audience gets your message and to give a certain depth and gravity to your words. Like music, repetition works at a fairly deep level on the audience's subconscious awareness of pattern and sound. The danger, as with all rhetorical techniques, is that it can be over-used and become predictable. Powerful repetition then becomes merely repetitious. Fiorina's second favourite technique is the use of contrast. The Comdex speech contains three contrasts (two of them quite subtle) – what FedEx, Amazon and BMW were told they could never do, but succeeded in doing anyway; the 'cynics and the doubters' who don't make any progress as opposed to those who do; the difficult economic climate which makes HP's work even more, not less, important. The Stanford speech contains two strong contrasts: what distinguishes successful from unsuccessful people; what courage is not and what it is.

b In the first speech a rhetorical question ('Why is this the face we have chosen to show the world?') marks a transition from talking about the focus of HP's ad campaign to the corporate philosophy behind it. Rhetorical questions can be very useful as a way of signalling a change of direction from one stage of a presentation to the next.
In the second speech a rhetorical question ('So what do I know about change?') is used to open the whole talk. This is a very quick way of getting straight to the point of the presentation without a lengthy introduction.

c Good public speakers instinctively vary the length of their sentences. A speech full of long complicated sentences is monotonous and difficult to follow. But a speech consisting only of short simple sentences rapidly begins to sound pretentious and over-dramatic. The secret is to alternate between the two. Two or three short sentences punctuated by one longer one will work well, but there's no need to stick to a pattern. In fact, a pattern is the last thing you want, for then you become predictable. See how Carly Fiorina does it.

d There are subtle differences between the two speeches. The informal Stanford speech contains more short sentences and this sets the conversational tone Fiorina aims to achieve. To overcome the potential distancing effect of the greater formality in the Comdex speech, Fiorina uses the first person plural no fewer than eleven times. In the Stanford speech she uses 'you' and 'I' more often to create the illusion of a dialogue. It's also interesting that whereas there are two groups of three in the Comdex speech, the Stanford speech contains none. Perhaps this rhetorical technique lends itself better to a more formal occasion than to a conversational one.

9A Storytelling

1

a Storytelling is a vital part of leadership – not only the charismatic kind of leadership that seeks to motivate and inspire, but also the quieter, more hands-off kind of leadership that seeks to guide and facilitate.
Leaders need to tell many kinds of stories – stories about successes and failures, about the past and the future, about people and plans, dreams and ambitions, good fortune and adversity, about lessons learned. Increasingly, leaders need to tell stories about change and corporate social responsibility.

b Stories are a powerful form of communication for anyone in business at all levels of the corporate hierarchy. Everyone can tell a basic story. If you can talk someone through your CV or talk about the history of your company, you can already tell a story, but you may need to work on improving your technique.
Frontline managers have a need to speak both up and down – up to their bosses and down to their subordinates. Getting buy-in for your ideas from people with more authority than you and who already know all the facts requires real skill. Stories can help here. Specialists of all kinds will often find it easier to explain what they are doing to non-specialists by avoiding jargon and technical terms and telling a story instead.

c The golden rules of storytelling are: make sure your story is relevant to the theme of your presentation; keep it short but not so short that your story lacks colour and detail, the things that bring it alive in the minds of your audience; don't rush the important parts of your story; pause before you deliver the really important parts; involve the audience through questions; use direct speech wherever you can. It's much more effective to hear what people in the story actually said and how they said it. Try to recreate the moment, not just report it.

2

a Create drama:
… all of a sudden the customer pulls out a gun and he says: 'This is a stick-up! Give me all the cash in the register!'

b Signal the end of the story:
You know what it said in the paper?

c Establish credibility:
By the way, this is a true story … Now, I'm not making this up. This was in the paper.

d Deliver the punchline:
'And the robber left satisfied.'

e Involve the audience:
Admiral, what would you do in that situation? … What would you do?

f Link to the theme of the presentation:
… My subject today is the courage to negotiate.

g Set the scene:
A couple of years ago, a man walks into a sandwich shop in Delray Beach, Florida and orders a meatball sandwich.

3

a The story itself is told entirely in the present simple. Brodow only uses the past simple to emphasise that he is relating exactly what happened as it was described in the newspaper. The present simple gives a sense of immediacy to his story. It gives the impression that the drama is unfolding as we listen. For simple anecdotes, the past simple will often suffice. But if your story is at all dramatic with plenty of dialogue and action, the present simple will often work better. When you set your story in the past, you make it more distant in time. But when you tell it in the present, you bring it right into the moment.

b Questions are the quickest and most effective way of involving your audience. They're useful in all parts of a presentation, not just for telling stories. In a story your questions will mostly be either rhetorical and require no answer ('You know what it said in the paper?') or semi-rhetorical, requiring just a short predictable answer that pushes the story along ('Admiral, what would you do in that situation? You'd give him the money. I sure would give him the money.')

c Again, it's about giving the story more immediate impact. Reporting speech removes it from the here and now. Quoting it is like replaying a recording of what actually happened. Compare 'He said he really wasn't interested' with 'So he says: "Look, forget it!"' By using the second version, the speaker makes you feel as if you're part of the story. It's the difference between someone describing a goal in a soccer match to you and watching the action replay.

d There are several examples of repetition. 'Meatball sandwich' is mentioned eight times. If the story had a title it would probably be called 'The Meatball Sandwich'. Variations on 'what would you do' and 'that's not what happened' are repeated too. Because of the amount of dialogue, we also get a lot of 'he says'. Repetition is great in a story because it makes the main points clear and easy to follow, but, even more importantly, it gives a rhythm and structure to the story. In fact, it makes it a story and not just a report. In a report too much repetition would be redundant, a sign of poor writing style. In a story it is key.

4

A couple of years ago, | a man walks into a sandwich shop in Delray Beach, Florida | and orders a meatball sandwich. | So the owner starts to fix the meatball sandwich | when all of a sudden the customer pulls out a gun

| and he says: 'This is a stick-up! | Give me all the cash in the register!' | Now, I don't know what you would do in a situation like that. | Admiral, | what would you do in that situation? | You'd give him the money. | I sure would give him the money. | What would you do? | You'd give him the money. | Well, | that's not what happened. | By the way, this is a true story. | That's not what happened. | The owner of the shop | puts down the meatball sandwich, | looks at the robber | and he says: | 'Listen, pal. | We've had a really bad month.' | He says: 'Business has been terrible. | Would you settle for ten dollars and the meatball sandwich?' | Now, I'm not making this up. | This was in the paper. | He says: 'Will you settle for ten dollars and the meatball sandwich?' | So the gunman says: 'Are you crazy?' | He says: 'I've got a gun here! | I'm not settling for ten dollars and the meatball sandwich.' | He says: 'I'm not settling for anything less than twenty dollars and the meatball sandwich!' | So, the owner says: | 'You got a deal!' | Gives him the twenty bucks, | gives him the meatball sandwich. | You know what it said in the paper? | It said: 'And the robber left satisfied.' | | ... My subject today | is the courage to negotiate.

6

Rapport: Stories are like a bridge between the presenter and the audience; they turn the presenter's experience into a movie the audience can play inside their heads

Timing: Keep your stories short; watch your audience as you tell them to see how you're doing

Humour: Stories can be funny, but they don't have to be; people don't have the same expectations of a story as they do of a joke; Western humour may not work in Asia, in any case

Credibility: Making fun of yourself is generally OK, but be careful not to make jokes about your area of expertise (if you're a corporate lawyer, you can make fun of your bad time management, but not about the day you lost your company a $10m court case!)

Influence: Stories are like the Trojan Horse; they are a good way of getting past audience resistance – especially if they are powerful, emotional stories

9B Storytelling

1

A story well told is a great way to arouse the interest of the audience. By the end of the story, they are ready, if they haven't already partially worked it out for themselves, to hear what the key message is and what facts and figures back it up. But, if you give them the facts first, then they already know why you're telling your story before you begin. You've spoilt the element of surprise. You're no longer exploiting your audience's natural curiosity to see the pieces fall into place. You've deprived them of their 'Aha!' moment.

2

True stories have a special appeal all of their own. If you tell a joke or a story about someone else, then it had better be good or your audience will wonder why you wasted their time telling it! But when you tell an anecdote, it's a window onto your experience and personality. As long as the story is relevant and not too long, you'll have your audience's attention. And if your anecdote reminds them of similar experiences they've had themselves, so much the better!

3

a The presenter begins by confessing to a failure that turned out well in the end. Asian audiences generally appreciate some sign of humility, especially in the young, so this is an effective opening strategy. Then she goes on to show that she started her business with next to nothing, working out of her apartment with no staff, and still managed to succeed. The audience laughs because it's something they can relate to, being young aspiring entrepreneurs themselves. This is a good example of a 'bonding story'. In effect, the speaker is saying to the audience: 'I know what it's like to be in your position, but it worked for me, and, if you work hard, it can work for you too.'

b The story of the guest satisfaction questionnaires is something any hotel manager can relate to. So the presenter begins with the familiar. He then does two things. First, he surprises his audience with some unexpected statistics. These turn a simple anecdote into a revealing piece of market research. From these statistics he draws his conclusion – customer satisfaction is not the same as customer loyalty. And to underline the validity of his conclusion he then draws an analogy between customers and life partners by asking his audience a direct question, which is also a joke. When they laugh at the joke, they are, in a way, also accepting that the point he is making is true – a clever use of humour to persuade.

c The subject of hiring more mature job applicants, who may have been out of the workforce for a while, is a potentially sensitive one. Such people may have a great deal of experience, but a lot of it could be out of date. When you hire college-leavers they know they have a lot to learn. But the older applicant may think they know it already, so they may have to 'unlearn' a lot of old skills before they can even start to learn new ones. In that sense, they could be harder to train than young recruits. So the speaker cleverly uses the self-effacing story of his own attempt to relearn tennis after 20 years to soften his message about recruiting older people. He does not himself work in HR, but he knows that an audience of HR directors is probably going to consist of slightly unfit middle-aged people like himself. So his anecdote also helps to break down any possible resistance to a professor trying to tell executives how to do their job.

4

Let your voice reflect the emotions in the story
Quote actual conversations
Use gestures to illustrate the story
Exaggerate your descriptions a little
Draw interesting comparisons
Stick to present tenses for greater impact
Involve the audience as you speak

5

a She looked up from her desk and **said: 'What do you want?'**
b He **said: 'To be honest, I don't know the first thing about computers.'**
c He **said: 'Don't interrupt me when I'm speaking!'**
d I **said: 'You've got to be joking!'**
e She took me to one side and **said: 'I have some information you might be interested in.'**
f He **said: 'I'm afraid that's not my job.'**

g She **said: 'Of course, you're the world's expert on customer relations, aren't you?'**
h He **said: 'I can't hear myself think!'**

6 *Suggested answers*

So I **come** out into the arrivals area at Charles de Gaulle airport and **there's** nobody waiting for me. I **wait** for about quarter of an hour, but still nobody **comes**. So I **ring** their office, but **there's** no answer. And **I'm** thinking to myself: **'This is very odd.'** Another 45 minutes **go** by. And now **I'm** really starting to panic. I mean, what **am** I supposed to do? **I'm** in a strange city. I **don't** know a soul. I **don't** even know which hotel **they've** booked me into – nothing. Finally – **I've** almost given up hope by this stage – this tall blonde woman **comes** up to me and **says: 'Are you Dr White?'** And I **say: 'Yes, I am. Where on earth have you been? I was beginning to think you'd forgotten me.'** And she **says: 'I'm very sorry! I was held up in traffic.'** It's not a great excuse, but, anyway, to cut a long story short, we **get** into a taxi and **head** into town, when suddenly she **turns** to me and **says: 'I'm really honoured to be working with one of America's top neurosurgeons!'** And I **say: 'But I'm not a neurosurgeon. I'm an automotive engineer!'** And she **says: 'But aren't you Dr White from New York Hospital?'** And I **say: 'I'm afraid not. I'm Dr White from Cleveland Trucks.'** She'd picked up the wrong Dr White!

7

a exhausted	k gorgeous
b starving	l hideous
c enormous	m spotless
d tiny	n filthy
e impossible	o bizarre
f freezing	p terrifying
g boiling	q hilarious
h brilliant	r fascinating
i superb	s astonishing
j lousy	t thrilling

(*Other options:* a worn out, shattered   b famished, ravenous c huge, vast, immense, gigantic, colossal   d minute, microscopic e hopeless   f icy, perishing g sweltering, scorching, roasting, baking   i excellent, wonderful, terrific, fabulous, splendid, magnificent, tremendous, fantastic, marvellous, outstanding   j awful, rotten, terrible, abysmal, dreadful, miserable k stunning, striking, dazzling, lovely

l revolting, gruesome   m immaculate n grimy, grubby   o weird, uncanny p petrifying   q hysterical   r riveting s amazing, astounding   t exhilarating, stimulating, electrifying)

9

a – k   b – g   c – l   d – j   e – h   f – i

10A Q&A sessions

3

a a **good** question
b a **difficult** question
c an **off-topic** question
d an **unnecessary** question
e a **multiple** question
f a **hostile** question

4

a a **good** question: **deal** with it straight away
b a **difficult** question: **define** it, then **deflect** it, **defer** it, **decline** to answer it or **disarm** the questioner by admitting you don't know
c an **off-topic** question: **define** it, then **defer** it or **deal** with it briefly
d an **unnecessary** question: **deal** with it
e a **multiple** question: **divide** it up, then **deal** with it step by step
f a **hostile** question: **defuse** it, then **deal** with it

5

There are some alternatives here because the question types are not mutually exclusive. A good question can also be difficult to answer; not all hostile questions are difficult to answer, etc. But suggested responses are below:

a good question: e, q
a difficult question: b, f, g, i, j, l, n, p, r
an off-topic question: a, k
an unnecessary question: d, o
a multiple question: c, h, m
a hostile question: treat as a difficult question – best options are l and r

6

a You're asking me whether we're planning to go public with this.
b You want to know if we're in a position to take on more work.
c You ask me how I see the market developing.
d You're wondering what our chances of success are.
e You'd like to know when the launch date is going to be.

7

a You're asking why this scale of investment was necessary.
b You'd like me to go through some of the figures again.
c You have some concerns about the timeframe.
d You'd like to look again at some of the advantages of the new system.
e You have a question about the management structure.
f You're not fully convinced of the benefits of the initiative.

10B Q&A sessions

5

a Asking a question yourself can be a good way to get the audience to start asking questions. But make sure it's the kind of question your audience might have asked! Check for nods amongst them. If they look blank, try again by saying: '... Or perhaps an even more important question is ...'
b Making a joke of it will often save embarrassment if you know your audience likes humour. As you've already learned, some of the best humour in a presentation is spontaneous. And some of the best spontaneous humour comes from awkward moments – which is why they are often nothing to be afraid of.
c Putting people briefly into pairs or groups to discuss the issues you've been presenting will often help them to formulate better questions. They can then ask them jointly, e.g. 'We were wondering what you thought about ...?'

6

a – e   b – c   c – h   d – b   e – f
f – j   g – d   h – i   i – a   j – g

7

Extract 1: c   e
Extract 2: b   h
Extract 3: j   d
Extract 4: a   g
Extract 5: f   i

Additional materials

1B Opening and closing

8 OPEN-AND-CLOSE PRESENTATION With your partner, choose one of the companies below and prepare to present your product or service to the rest of your group, who are your prospective clients. One of you should open the presentation and the other should close it. In your opener, try to use some of the techniques you have studied to:

- capture your audience's attention
- tell them what's in it for them
- establish your credibility and expertise
- preview some of the features and benefits of the product or service.

Then, miss out the main body of the presentation and fast forward to your conclusion to:

- briefly summarise your main points
- explain what you'd like your audience to do
- close in a memorable way.

See if you can perhaps link your opening to your close to create a 'loop'. And try to avoid the word 'summary'!

Cocoon MRI Systems

Magnetic resonance imaging is a standard diagnostic tool in today's hospitals. But for many patients having to lie perfectly still in an MRI scanner for up to half an hour at a time can be highly stressful. For such patients the Cocoon creates a calming virtual environment. The fully customisable system provides a wide range of relaxing ambient settings – from rainforest to coral reef to Himalayan snow peak. Ceiling-mounted 3D video screens and surround-sound audio capability leave the patient feeling totally rested and refreshed at the end of their scan. That's the Cocoon experience.

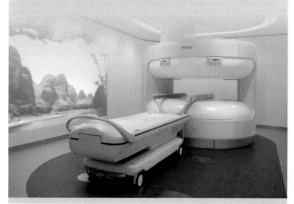

The Avenir Consultancy

The Avenir Consultancy is your company's access point to a network of some of the world's largest databases of global business intelligence. Working with one of our expert scenario planners and Avenir's own highly sophisticated computer simulation software, plot the trends likely to affect your business over the next decade, explore different commercial, economic and political scenarios and get a detailed digital profile of your company ten years into the future! Take strategic planning to the next level. At Avenir we have a word for it. We call it Tomorrow-ology.

Smart Fabrix Inc.

Using microscopic LEDs and cutting-edge fibre-technology, SmartFabrix has designed a range of light-emitting garments that can display multi-coloured graphics and animations without compromising wearability. By linking the luminous clothing to a PC or smartphone visuals can be modified to suit the wearer's mood and keep up with the latest urban fashions. Commercial applications include programming promotional messages into the clothes to turn their wearers into highly effective walking advertisements! Just follow the light.

Uneedanerd.com

More than just an IT support service or helpline, a year's subscription to uneedanerd.com provides you with an instant videoconferencing link from your PC or Mac to 'nerd central' where our resident nerds will sort out computer problems big or small online on a pay-per-solution basis, offer impartial advice on hardware and software selection or even coach you in the use of the latest Web 2.0 and multimedia applications. In a full-scale emergency a nerd crash-team is on call 24/7. You need a nerd? You need us!

2A Smooth structure

5 THE SIGNPOST MAZE **Work with a partner. You are going to play a game to practise using signpost language.**

Enter the maze below and take it in turns to speak using the signpost notes to help you. One of you should take the grey squares and the other the blue. Follow the arrows until you reach the exit. Then swap squares and see if you can find a different route.

If you can't think of what to say, you lose a point!

Once you're used to the game, try just looking at the notes in each square as you play and then standing up to speak.

The situation is: a presenter is reporting to his/her superiors on an intercultural project he/she is involved in.

ENTER

Then ● like ● talk you through ● main phases ● project	First ● briefly ● going ● give ● some background	Like ● start off ● outlining ● main goals today	First of all ● going ● give ● brief overview ● project	Then ● like ● fill you in ● some ● details
But before ● start ● let ● ask ● question	Let's move on ● subject ● planning	Turning ● moment ● question ● schedules	Moving on ● some ● initial problems ● faced	By ● end ● talk ● hope ● clearer idea ● progress ● made so far
So ● next question ● how did ● deal ● cultural differences?	If ● could just digress ● moment here	Just ● return ● main point ● a minute	This leads us ● question ● virtual teams	Perhaps ● should just expand ● that a little
We'll ● coming on ● this later	Going back ● what ● saying earlier	I'll ● saying more ● this later on	This brings us ● question ● budgeting	Like ● take ● moment ● talk ● logistics
Closing ● just like ● summarise ● some ● main points ● looked at	OK, well ● brings me ● end ● presentation ● thanks very much	Conclusion ● general ● been ● very successful project	OK, so ● looked ● logistics ● let's finish ● talking ● next phase	Any questions ● like ● ask ● this point?

EXIT

2B Smooth structure

8 PRESENTATION TEMPLATE Work individually or with a partner. Use the template to develop a short presentation with a strong opening, a strong ending and three main stages in between.

Make a note of:

- the main points you want to make in the white boxes
- key topic vocabulary you think you may need in the yellow boxes
- expressions that may help you at each stage of the presentation (e.g. 'One option may be …', 'In the long term …') in the grey boxes
- signpost language to transition from one stage to the next (e.g. 'To move on', 'Turning to the question of financing, …') in the green boxes.

Possible stages:

problem-solving (*problem, options, recommendations*)

product / service description (*features, benefits, competitor comparison*)

common misconception (*myth, data, reality*)

business plan (*customer need, idea, market potential*)

troubleshooting (*problem, possible causes, action*)

change (*past, present, implications*)

motivation (*competition, us, future*)

proposal (*plan, potential objections, benefits*)

financial / sales report (*targets, results, implications*)

company timeline (*past, present, future*)

directive from head office (*issue, decision, implications*)

manufacturing process / research procedure (*aims, procedure, results*)

pitch for (*increased*) resources (*need, plan, costs*)

departmental profile (*team, areas of activity, current projects*)

situation report (*past, present, causes*)

market overview (*market profile, trends and market forces, market share*).

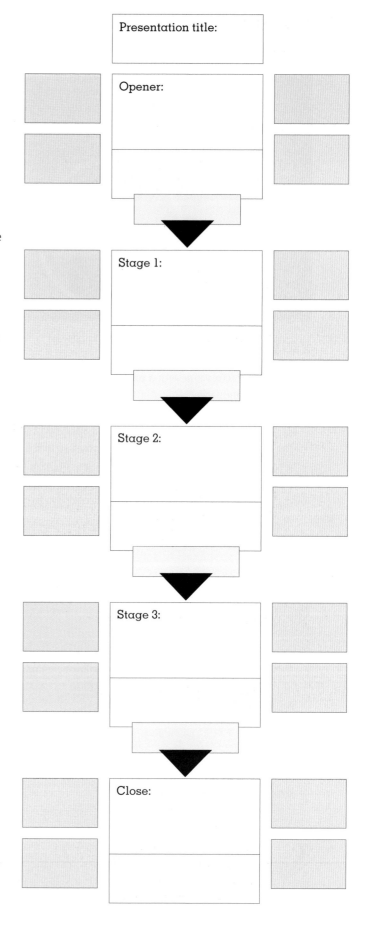

3B Voice power

2 SPEECH OPENERS

Change

As management guru Tom Peters once said,

'If you don't like change, you're going to like irrelevance even less.'

Risk

As British financier Sir James Goldsmith once said,

'The ultimate risk is not taking a risk.'

Simplicity

As Albert Einstein once said,

'Everything should be made as simple as possible – but not simpler.'

The future

As communication expert Marshall McLuhan once said,

'Tomorrow is our permanent address.'

Intellectual capital

As management guru Peter Drucker once said,

'From now on the key is knowledge.'

Opportunity

As the president of Mitsubishi, Minoru Makihara, once said,

'Where there are changes, there is opportunity.'

Collaboration

As web gurus Dan Tapscott and Anthony Williams once said,

'We must collaborate or perish.'

Leadership

As re-engineering guru Michael Hammer once said,

'Without leadership, nothing happens.'

Social responsibility

As the financier Jim Slater once said,

'I personally believe that capitalism, as it is now, won't survive unless it becomes more socially responsible.'

Competition

As the managing director of Rank Xerox, Vernon Zelmer, once said,

'If you have found a way to do something in two steps, you can be sure that someone in the Far East has found a way to do it in one.'

7 Sᴏᴜɴᴅ-ꜱᴄʀɪᴘᴛɪɴɢ Follow the step-by-step instructions to sound-script the opening or closing minute of a presentation you might give. Then use your sound-script to deliver your speech to the rest of your group.

a

In the days before advertising there was word of mouth. Products and services that worked simply got talked about and eventually we bought them. Then came advertising and billions were spent by marketing departments to achieve the same thing. Today we're back where we started – only today it's called word of web. And it's a whole lot faster.

> Type out a short section of your presentation in full – perhaps the opening or the conclusion.

b

In the days before advertising
there was word of mouth.
Products and services
that worked
simply got talked about
and eventually
we bought them.
Then came advertising
and billions were spent
by marketing departments
to achieve the same thing.
Today
we're back where we started
– only today
it's called word of web.
And it's a whole
lot
faster.

> Run your cursor through the text and press **RETURN** where you'd like to pause.

c

In the **days** before **advertising**
there was **word** of **mouth**.
Products and **services**
that **worked**
simply got **talked about**
and **eventually**
we **bought them**.
Then came **advertising**
and **billions** were **spent**
by **marketing departments**
to **achieve** the same **thing**.
Today
we're **back** where we **started**
– only **today**
it's called **word** of **web**.
And it's a **whole**
lot
faster.

> Decide which words should be stressed and put them in **bold**.

d

In the **days** before **advertising**
there was **word** of **mouth**.
Products and **services**
that **worked**
simply got **talked about**
and **eventually**
we **bought them**.
Then came **advertising**
and **billions** were **spent**
by **marketing departments**
to **achieve** the same **thing**.
Today
we're **back** where we **started**
– only **today**
it's called **word** of **web**.
And it's a **whole**
lot
faster.

> If you want to, you can put unstressed words into a smaller font.

e

In the **days** before **advertising** ↑
there was **word** of **mouth**. ↓
Products and **services** ↑
that **worked** ↑
simply got **talked about** ↓
and **eventually** ↑
we **bought them**. ↓
Then came **advertising** ↓
and **billions** were **spent** ↑
by **marketing departments** ↑
to **achieve** the same **thing**. ↓
Today ↑
we're **back** where we **started** ↓
– only **today** ↑
it's called **word** of **web**. ↓
And it's a **whole** ↑
lot ↑
faster. ↓

> Optionally, you could mark the intonation with arrows (↑↓) at the end of each line.

f

In the **days** before **advertising** ↑
there was **word** of **mouth**. ↓
Products and **services** ↑
that **worked** ↑
simply got **talked about** ↓
and **eventually** ↑
we **bought them**. ↓
Then came **advertising** ↓
and **billions** were **spent** ↑
by **marketing departments** ↑
to **achieve** the same **thing**. ↓
Today ↑
we're **back** where we **started** ↓
– only **today** ↑
it's called **word** of **web**. ↓
And it's a **whole** ↑
lot ↑
faster. ↓

> To get a sense of what you can do with your voice, highlight louder and quieter sections.

4A Visual aids

8 BEFORE AND AFTER How successfully do you think the designer has improved the slides?

Before

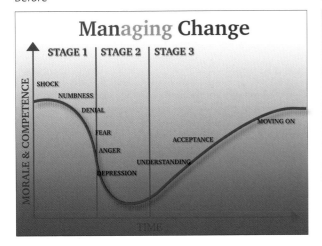

After

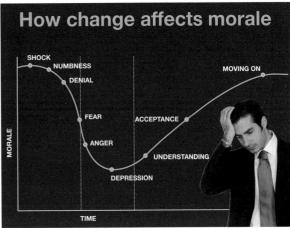

The text is gradually revealed as the presenter speaks using 'custom animation'.

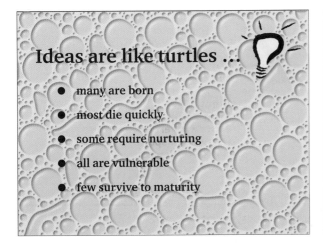

The text is revealed in two parts as the presenter speaks using 'custom animation'.

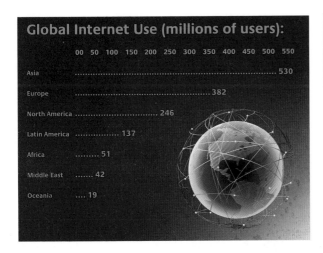

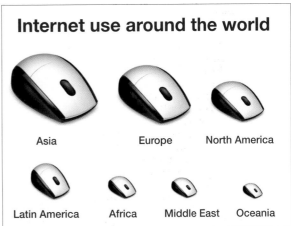

4B Visual aids

10 S<small>TATS BANK</small>

1 Work individually or with a partner. Choose one of the sets of statistics from the Stats bank below (or choose some figures of your own) and prepare to present them to the rest of your group.

2 Things to consider as you prepare:

- what your key message is and how much of the data you want to display
- what sort of graph (if any) would work best: a line graph, bar chart, pie chart, etc.
- what kind of visual image (if any) you need to support the text
- whether to use bullet points
- whether you want to project the whole slide at once or use animation to gradually reveal different parts of it
- whether images could be used to replace parts of the text
- whether any special effects would be helpful
- whether audio or video would be worth adding.

3 When you're ready, either:
– talk through your idea without any visual support or make a rough sketch of your visual aid design and explain how it would work to the rest of your group
or:
– actually produce your visual aid in PowerPoint or Apple Keynote and present it to the rest of your group.

Average Household TV Viewing (Hrs per day)

USA	8
Turkey	5
Italy	4
UK	3
Switzerland	2½

Top Five Debtor Nations

US (–$800 bn), Spain (–$160 bn), UK (–$105 bn), Australia (–$55 bn), France (–$50 bn)

Top Five Creditor Nations

China (+$450 bn), Japan (+$195 bn), Germany (+$170 bn), Saudi Arabia (+$80 bn), Switzerland (+$65 bn)

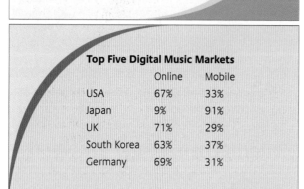

Top Five Digital Music Markets

	Online	Mobile
USA	67%	33%
Japan	9%	91%
UK	71%	29%
South Korea	63%	37%
Germany	69%	31%

Average Annual Sick Leave (No. days per employee)

Bulgaria – 22
Portugal – 12
Norway – 10
France – 8½
Germany – 6½
Turkey – 4½
USA – 4

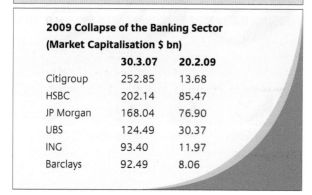

2009 Collapse of the Banking Sector (Market Capitalisation $ bn)

	30.3.07	20.2.09
Citigroup	252.85	13.68
HSBC	202.14	85.47
JP Morgan	168.04	76.90
UBS	124.49	30.37
ING	93.40	11.97
Barclays	92.49	8.06

World Population Growth

10000 BC	0.005 bn	AD 1800	0.9 bn
1000 BC	0.05 bn	AD 1950	2.5 bn
0	0.17 bn	AD 2000	6 bn
AD 1000	0.25 bn	AD 2050	9 bn
AD 1500	0.4 bn		

5A Facts and figures

6   Number game Work in groups of four, each using one of the data cards below. Speaker 1 should start by reading out their first number. Whoever has that number should cross it out and read out the next number on their card (crossing that out too). Whoever has that number should cross that out and read out the next and so on until Speaker 1 reads out the final number on their card.

Each speaker only has five seconds in which to cross out the number they have just heard and read the next on their card. See how far through the game you can get without hesitation or mistakes and give your team one point for each correctly presented figure.

Speaker 1	Speaker 2
0.01%	6¾
$313.30	2011
90°	90°
€17,770	Q1–4
½%	¥6.9 bn
22cc	6,000 rpm
£12.75	▲ 2¼ pts
5,893,619	5,893,619
$68,000 pa	01.07.09
1Gb	10Mb
$23 tr	$23 tr
911,677,803	ISO 4217

Speaker 3	Speaker 4
0.01%	2011
6¾	$313.30
6:1	Q1–4
€17,770	6:1
6,000 rpm	½%
22cc	¥6.9 bn
101 sqm	£12.75
▲ 2¼ pts	101 sqm
$68,000 pa	10Mb
01.07.09	1Gb
ISO 4217	▼ ⅞%
▼ ⅞%	911,677,803

5B Facts and figures

9   Talking figures Work individually or with a partner. Choose a graph from the selection below and on page 86 and memorise as much of the accompanying information as you can. When you're ready, present the graph to the rest of your group. Try to make sure you:

- focus on just the most significant data
- articulate the key figures well
- use round figures wherever possible
- make larger figures meaningful by setting them in context
- describe any trends or developments accurately.

Putting out fire with gasoline

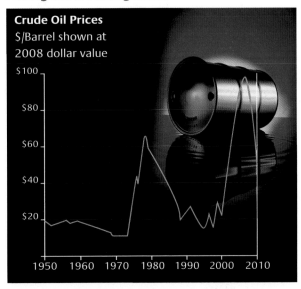

Crude Oil Prices
$/Barrel shown at 2008 dollar value

Notes

Oil prices seem to be a remarkably accurate barometer of the general political and economic climate – almost quarter of a century of steadily declining oil prices (apart from Suez Crisis in 1956) – peak of 80–81 caused by Yom Kippur War oil embargo (73), Iranian Revolution (79) and Iran–Iraq War (80) – smaller peaks of 1990 and 1999 due to Gulf War and OPEC cuts respectively – all-time high of 2008 (just falling short of the $100-a-barrel threshold) a result of 9/11 (01), the invasion of Iraq (03), Venezuelan strikes (03–05), and a weak dollar – collapses of 81, 89 and 08 due to global recessions – the question is: are the fluctuations, like the world, getting more violent?

Anything for an easy life

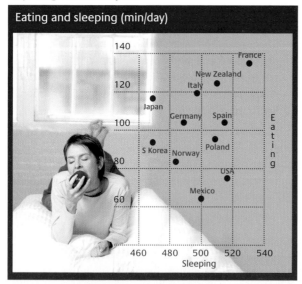

Eating and sleeping (min/day)

(France, New Zealand, Italy, Japan, Germany, Spain, S Korea, Norway, Poland, USA, Mexico — plotted against Sleeping 460, 480, 500, 520, 540 and Eating 60, 80, 100, 120, 140)

Notes

Today's high-pressure world gives us all little time for a decent night's sleep and a relaxing meal, but cultural behaviour patterns vary significantly – within the group of mostly rich OECD nations, the French spend longest wining, dining and resting (well over 2hrs eating, nearly 9hrs sleeping) – Americans too get plenty of rest, but along with their neighbours, the Mexicans, tend to 'eat on the run' – the more frenetic work cultures of Japan and South Korea survive on an hour's sleep less than the French, but still get well over 7hrs – in Italy food takes precedence over sleep – what the figures don't show is the prevalence in the developed West of sleep disturbances, poor nutrition and eating disorders.

Live long and prosper?

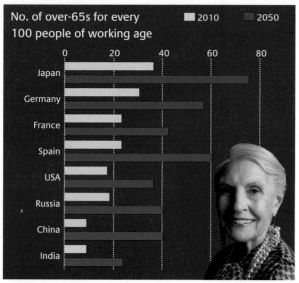

No. of over-65s for every 100 people of working age

■ 2010 ■ 2050

(Japan, Germany, France, Spain, USA, Russia, China, India; scale 0, 20, 40, 60, 80)

Notes

It's well known that, thanks to improved health care and falling birth rates, the developed world's population is ageing, but the figures highlight some important variations in the trend – by 2050 Japan, Spain and Germany will be amongst the most dramatically affected – in Japan over-65s will equal around ¾ of the working population – in all three countries this will place an enormous tax burden on the declining number of working young – India's elderly will more than double too, but still only equal about ¼ of the workforce – this could mean a brain-drain of talented young workers to the West – but in China the number of elderly will quadruple to 40% and that may lead to a substantial fall in productivity.

Raising energy levels

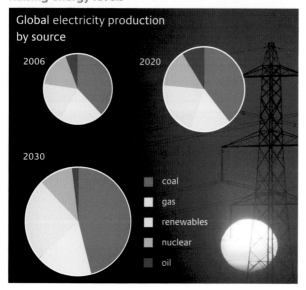

Global electricity production by source

2006 2020 2030

■ coal
■ gas
■ renewables
■ nuclear
■ oil

Notes

Increased investment in renewable energy (solar, wind, hydro, biomass and waste, tide and wave) is a positive response to population increase and rising fossil-fuel prices – in 2006 renewables comprised approximately 18% of electricity sources; by 2030 that figure will be 23% (predominantly, hydro and wind power) – by contrast, reliance on nuclear energy and oil will have declined significantly – but is this good news? – nuclear energy is at least clean – by 2030 electricity production will have doubled and 44% of it will still be derived from coal, the dirtiest source – solar energy is unlikely to really come on stream till 2040 – so where's our greener, more sustainable future?

6B Body language

10 BODY LANGUAGE Use the template below when you are preparing your presentation.

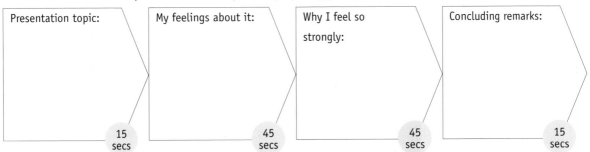

Presentation topic:	My feelings about it:	Why I feel so strongly:	Concluding remarks:
15 secs	45 secs	45 secs	15 secs

7A Rapport building

7 CONTROVERSIAL IDEAS You're going to give a three-minute presentation of a controversial idea. Your objective is to persuade your audience that your idea, though it may seem ridiculous at first, is right. Try to use some of the rapport language you've been practising (first person plural, question tags, negative question forms, involvement expressions) to make your speech more persuasive.

Here's a basic template to help you prepare:

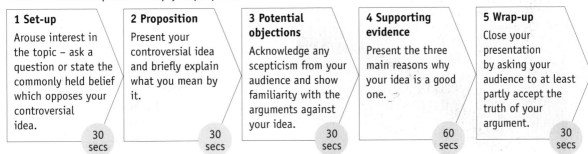

1 Set-up
Arouse interest in the topic – ask a question or state the commonly held belief which opposes your controversial idea.
30 secs

2 Proposition
Present your controversial idea and briefly explain what you mean by it.
30 secs

3 Potential objections
Acknowledge any scepticism from your audience and show familiarity with the arguments against your idea.
30 secs

4 Supporting evidence
Present the three main reasons why your idea is a good one.
60 secs

5 Wrap-up
Close your presentation by asking your audience to at least partly accept the truth of your argument.
30 secs

And here are some suggestions for controversial ideas you could present:

Controversial ideas bank

If what you're doing is working, try something else.

A happy workforce is an unproductive workforce.

Try hiring people you don't like for a change.

Always judge a book by its cover.

If you don't look anything like your customers, something is seriously wrong.

Routinely disobey your boss.

There's no dividing line between products and services.

Work as if you were going to be a lifetime employee of the same company.

You're only a leader if other people say you are.

Globalisation is a myth.

In business, big is still beautiful.

Stop working. Start playing.

Dreams have zero value. Anyone can dream.

Recession can be a very good thing.

The customer is not always king.

90% of the time mediocrity is good enough.

Success is a bigger problem than failure.

7B Rapport building

6 THE CRAZY INVENTION Chindogu is the Japanese art of inventing ingenious gadgets which, in solving a common everyday problem, unfortunately create an even bigger problem! Work with a partner to team-present one of the Chindogu products below to the rest of your group, who are department store buyers.

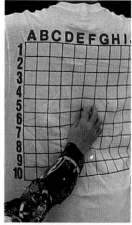
Backscratcher T-shirt

Personal tissue-dispenser

Baby floor-polisher

Noodle-cooler

Butter-stick

Umbrella tie

Things you might include in your 5-minute presentation are:

* identification of a common need or problem
* previous unsuccessful attempts to meet that need or solve that problem
* how your invention successfully meets the need or solves the problem
* basic product features and operating procedure
* optional extras
* your target market
* prices, availability, delivery, etc.

You already have a humorous product to present, but try to build in extra humour with funny quotes, visuals or prepared 'spontaneous' remarks. Also try to address different intelligence types using:

* visuals
* puzzles
* handouts
* audio and video
* reflective activities
* discussion activities

Obviously, you don't need to use all these techniques in one presentation! But prepare to build in one or two.

8A Impact techniques

8 SPEECHWRITING With a partner, rewrite the short presentation extract below so that it contains more repetition of words, phrases and sounds. You may need to break some of it up into shorter sentences. Change or add whatever you need to. Then team-present your rewritten presentation, emphasising the words and phrases you decided to repeat. Listen and compare your version with the one on the CD (CD2.12).

There'll always be a market for quality. And that's what I want to talk to you about this morning. So what do I know about it? Three things: it's better, it costs more and, importantly, people actually want it to cost extra. It's not about your goods; it's about how people perceive your goods. As Stella Artois's clever beer ad used to put it: 'Reassuringly expensive'. I don't know a better definition of quality.

8B Impact techniques

9 SPEECHWRITING With a partner, rewrite the notes about baby boomers as a presentation using as many impact techniques as you can. Then team-present your rewritten presentation. Listen and compare your version with the one on the CD (CD2.16).

8C Impact techniques

6 SUPERCHARGING YOUR PRESENTATION

1 Work with a partner. Look at the presentation extracts below and increase their impact by:
   - replacing neutral adjectives with more vivid alternatives (a–f)
   - adding intensifiers (g–j)
   - switching contrasts around (k–m)
   - using metaphors and images (n–p)

   There are hints to help you.

2 Try delivering some of the extracts in front of your group. Think especially about pausing and emphasis.

Booming baby boomers

Marketers traditionally concentrate on 18–44-year-olds (fashion-conscious, media-aware, comfortable with technology, responsive to advertising) – tend to ignore so-called 'baby boomers' (generation born between 1946 and 1964) – over-60s = 20% of US population (up from 12% in 1950) – now more Italians over 60 than under 20 – by 2050 40% of Japanese will be over 60 – over-60s have a lot of disposable income and a lot of free time to spend it – also living longer – in USA families headed by over-40s = 99% of country's net worth – boomers don't want to be treated like overgrown kids – don't want to be treated like geriatrics – know they're getting older, but don't want to 'get old' – big opportunities in travel and tourism, adventure holidays, luxury vehicles, health and fitness, cosmetic and spare-part surgery – boomers want experiences they missed the first time round.

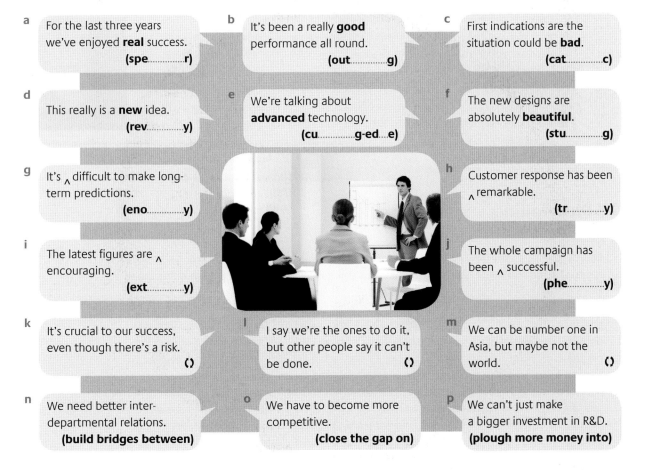

a For the last three years we've enjoyed **real** success. (spe.............r)

b It's been a really **good** performance all round. (out.............g)

c First indications are the situation could be **bad**. (cat.............c)

d This really is a **new** idea. (rev.............y)

e We're talking about **advanced** technology. (cu.............g-ed...e)

f The new designs are absolutely **beautiful**. (stu.............g)

g It's ∧ difficult to make long-term predictions. (eno.............y)

h Customer response has been ∧ remarkable. (tr.............y)

i The latest figures are ∧ encouraging. (ext.............y)

j The whole campaign has been ∧ successful. (phe.............y)

k It's crucial to our success, even though there's a risk. ( )

l I say we're the ones to do it, but other people say it can't be done. ( )

m We can be number one in Asia, but maybe not the world. ( )

n We need better inter-departmental relations. (**build bridges between**)

o We have to become more competitive. (**close the gap on**)

p We can't just make a bigger investment in R&D. (**plough more money into**)

8D Impact techniques

7 PRESENTING USING IMPACT TECHNIQUES Work with a partner to design a short team-presentation using some of the many different techniques you've studied to add impact.

1 Choose a presentation topic with the simple title: X is …

(Examples: Success is …, Happiness is …, Creativity is …, Innovation is …, Quality is …, Service is …, Technology is …, Professionalism is …, Globalisation is …, Equal opportunity is …, Fair competition is …, etc.)

2 Decide if you are going to make your presentation more formal or informal.

3 Draft your speech incorporating impact techniques where you can to make it more effective.

4 Now reduce your presentation to brief notes on prompt cards.

5 Rehearse giving your presentation using your prompt cards. Only refer to the full text of your speech if you need to.

6 Deliver your presentation with your partner, again using your prompt cards to keep you on track.

9A Storytelling

7 STORYTELLING

Student A
Read the story below and reduce it to ten key words or fewer. Then retell the story to a partner in your own way. What subject do you think the speaker's presentation is going to be about? Try to link up to that subject at the end of the story.

> There's a misconception that you're either creative or you're not and there's not much you can do about it. Everybody has immense creative capacities. I heard a great story about this of a teacher who was taking a drawing lesson with a group of six-year-old girls. And one of these girls, she was completely absorbed in what she was doing for about half an hour. The teacher said: 'What are you drawing?' And the girl said: 'I'm drawing a picture of God.' And the teacher said: 'But nobody knows what God looks like.' And the little girl said: 'They will in a minute!' At that age children have immense confidence in their own conceptions. But ten years later they've lost that.
>
> *Sir Ken Robinson, author and educator*

9B Storytelling

6 STORYTELLING

So I came out into the arrivals area at Charles de Gaulle airport and there was nobody waiting for me. I waited for about quarter of an hour, but still nobody came. So I rang their office, but there was no answer. And I was thinking to myself that this was very odd. Another 45 minutes went by. And now I was really starting to panic. I mean, what was I supposed to do? I was in a strange city. I didn't know a soul. I didn't even know which hotel they'd booked me into – nothing. Finally – I'd almost given up hope by this stage – this tall blonde woman came up to me and asked me if I was Dr White. And I said I was, asked her where on earth she'd been and told her I was beginning to think they'd forgotten me. And she said she was very sorry. She was held up in traffic. It's not a great excuse, but, anyway, to cut a long story short, we got into a taxi and headed into town, when suddenly she turned to me and said how honoured she was to be working with one of America's top neurosurgeons. And I said that I wasn't a neurosurgeon. I was an automotive engineer. And she asked me if I was Dr White from New York Hospital. And I said I was afraid I wasn't. I was Dr White from Cleveland Trucks. She'd picked up the wrong Dr White!

10 DO-IT-YOURSELF ANECDOTE

Think of a time when:

- you've learned a valuable lesson (perhaps from a mistake)
- someone said something clever, enlightening or profound to you
- you've misjudged someone (positively or negatively)
- you've been surprised (pleasantly or unpleasantly)
- you've been amused or entertained (by something someone said or did)
- you've succeeded at something in spite of difficulties
- you've reached an important milestone in your career.

Does it make a good story? Could you link it to a presentation theme? Tell a short anecdote about it using some of the expressions you've worked with to structure and add emphasis to your story. Don't forget to incorporate:

- dialogue
- tone of voice
- gestures
- a little bit of exaggeration

into your story, if you can, and when you present it, try to involve your audience as much as possible. The template below may help you:

9A Storytelling

7 STORYTELLING

Student B

Read the story below and reduce it to ten key words or fewer. Then retell the story to a partner in your own way. What subject do you think the speaker's presentation is going to be about? Try to link up to that subject at the end of the story.

I come from a culture where the three highest superlatives are: 'Pretty good', 'Rather nice' or 'Not bad'. The difficulty of impressing us as customers is brought home by the story of an elderly lady who had never been to the sea. A well-meaning friend took her on a lengthy drive to witness this marvel. She stood on the shore for some time, gazing intently at the incoming tide, then turned to her host with the words: 'Is that all it does?' For all the effort that most organisations claim to put into creating great service for their customers, all too often 'Is that all you do?' is the most likely response. It's increasingly hard to 'wow' us.

Nigel Barlow, customer service expert

Begin story	Set context	Involve audience	Add emphasis	End story
Talking of …	This was about … years ago now.	Do you know what I mean?	But the really … thing was …	Anyway, to cut a long story short.
I'll never forget the (first) time I …	I guess this must have been around the time of …	You're not going to believe this, but …	But that was the least of it!	It turned out in the end that …
This reminds me of (the time) when …	I was living in / working for … at the time.	Can you imagine?	And that's not all!	So, in the end what happened was …
Did I (ever) tell you about the time I …?	Just before this I'd been … *ing*	How can I describe it (to you)?	But wait a minute. It gets better / worse.	So, anyway, finally, …
Let me tell you the story of how …	And in those days …	You should have heard / seen …	And to top it all, …	
		And you'll never guess what / who / where / how …		

10A Q&A sessions

8 THE STOPWATCH GAME

1 You are going to take part in a Q&A game. Imagine you work in the automotive industry and have just given or attended a presentation concerning a proposed joint venture with a foreign competitor to develop a new hybrid electric vehicle.

2 Work with a partner. Take it in turns to check what number the second hand is pointing to on your watch and then read out the question next to that number below. Begin each question by saying: 'Excuse me, I have a question.'

3 If it's a neutral question, your partner should just repeat it back to you. But if it's hostile (marked in red), they should try to rephrase it more neutrally. It's OK to ask the same question twice. Remember, you don't need to actually answer the questions. Just see how quickly and effectively you can respond!

46–48	Where would the engines be manufactured?	**1–3**	Could you just go over the project timeline again?
49–51	Aren't you underestimating the cultural problems?	**4–6**	Have you budgeted for possible project overruns?
52–54	Can you tell us how far you've got with R&D?	**7–9**	Why can't you give us a complete cost breakdown?
55–57	Are you honestly expecting the go-ahead today?	**10–12**	Who would be responsible for the design of the vehicles?
58–60	Can you show us the sales forecasts again?	**13–15**	How can you justify the enormous risks involved in this?
31–33	You realise we have zero experience in this sector?	**16–18**	Would you recommend keeping production in-house?
34–36	Could you just clarify your position on marketing?	**19–21**	Surely you're not suggesting we import components?
37–39	Can I ask you who would own the patents?	**22–24**	Do we have the right level of technical expertise?
40–42	Aren't you overlooking the competition?	**25–27**	How would this venture affect our existing business?
43–45	How much market research have you done?	**28–30**	If this is such a great idea, why haven't we done it before?

9 THE HOT-SEAT GAME

1 Work in groups. Each of you should prepare a 2-minute talk on a subject you know quite a lot about. It shouldn't be too technical unless you are working with people in the same business as you. It could just be something very simple like a hobby or an interest.

2 Take turns 'in the hot seat' and give your talks. Present slowly and clearly and make sure you introduce and structure your presentation properly.

3 The other people in your group should each ask at least three of the six types of question you've studied:

- A good question, e.g. ask for more information, raise an interesting related issue

- A difficult question, e.g. ask something very technical, perhaps for an exact figure
- An off-topic question, e.g. ask about something which has no connection with the talk
- An unnecessary question, e.g. ask for something that the presenter has already mentioned
- A multiple question, e.g. ask two or three separate questions at the same time
- A hostile question, e.g. ask something that contradicts the presenter or questions their credibility

They should interrupt you to ask their questions as you speak. Try to deal with each question in an appropriate way.

10B Q&A sessions

8 QUESTION MAZE

1 Work with a partner. Choose a subject you both know well and prepare six or seven questions each on the topic.

2 Now enter the maze below, taking turns to be the presenter and questioner. The questioner's instructions are in the grey boxes and the presenter's in the blue boxes. Use the questions you prepared to conduct your Q&A and follow the arrows until you reach the exit. See how many different routes you can find.

ENTER				
Correct the presenter's understanding of your question.	Repeat the question back to the questioner.	Ask a question.	Say you don't understand.	Rephrase the question.
Say you cannot answer now and say why.	Confirm that's what you're asking.	Answer the question and check the questioner is satisfied.	Rephrase the question.	Apologise. Say you still don't understand.
Push for an answer.	Say you don't know the answer.	Accept. Ask another question.	Say that raises a different issue.	Push for an answer.
Restate your position.	Accept and thank.	Offer to find out the answer.	Accept. Ask another question.	Restate your position.

EXIT

9 THE LAST Q&A

1 Look again at the presentation you prepared in **1–3** on page 48 and prepare to give it in full. If you can, design a few visuals to support you.

2 The rest of your group should listen to your presentation and take notes on questions they want to ask. Hold a Q&A session at the end. Questioners should properly contextualise their questions before asking them. Presenters should repeat or rephrase the questions before answering them. The question-generator below may help you:

CONTEXT ►	ZOOM IN ►	QUESTION
When you were ...	**You ...**	**Could you just ...**
talking about	mentioned	... elaborate / expand on that ? ■ ... say a bit more about that? ■ ... give us an example of what you mean? ■ ... tell us how you arrived at that figure? ■ ... go over that again (in more detail)?
telling us about	spoke about	
describing	referred to	
presenting	suggested	
outlining	questioned	Do you have any data to support that? ■ Are you in a position to tell us whether ...? ■ Where did you get your information on ...? ■ Have you done any research into ...? ■ How can you be (so) sure that ...? ■ Have you taken account of ...? ■ How would you respond to the criticism that ...? ■ How do you propose to deal with / solve the problem of ...? ■ Have you thought about what might happen if ...? ■ Aren't you overlooking the fact that ...?
considering	emphasised	
discussing	recommended	
dealing with	gave the impression	
evaluating	made the point that	
explaining	quoted a figure of	
summarising	showed us a slide	

Online feedback forms

As you work through *Dynamic Presentations* you'll be given frequent opportunities to practise your existing presentation skills and try out new ones. Each training session culminates in a longer speaking activity and, ideally, these should be audio-recorded or filmed for feedback.

On the dedicated website (http://www.cambridge.org/elt/dynamicpresentations/) you'll find detailed feedback forms for each module of the course, which you can print out for use – see thumbnails below.

Keep a record of your performance throughout the course and you'll be able to monitor your progress and establish where your personal strengths as a presenter lie. These, of course, are what you should draw on every time you present.

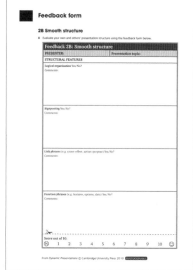
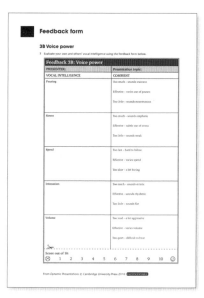
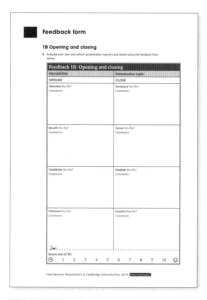
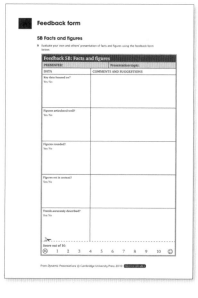

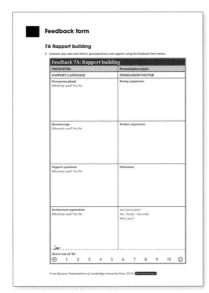

Feedback form

7A Rapport building

7 Evaluate your own and others' persuasiveness and rapport using the feedback form below.

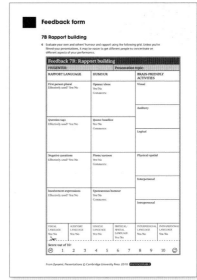

Feedback form

7B Rapport building

6 Evaluate your own and others' humour and rapport using the following grid. Unless you've filmed your presentations, it may be easier to get different people to concentrate on different aspects of your performance.

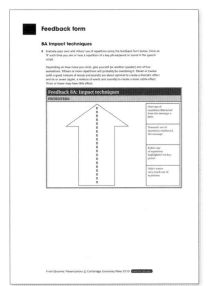

Feedback form

8A Impact techniques

8 Evaluate your own and others' use of repetition using the feedback form below. Circle an 'R' each time you see or hear a repetition of a key phrase/word or sound in the speech script.

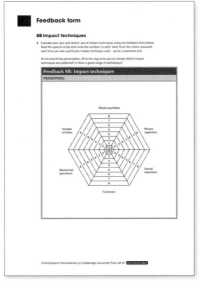

Feedback form

8B Impact techniques

9 Evaluate your own and others' use of impact techniques using the feedback form below. Read the speech script and circle the numbers in each 'slice' from the centre outwards each time you see a particular impact technique used – up to a maximum of 8.

Feedback form

8D Impact techniques

7 Evaluate your own and others' use of impact techniques using the feedback form below.

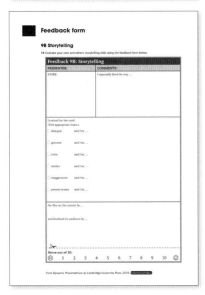

Feedback form

9B Storytelling

10 Evaluate your own and others' storytelling skills using the feedback form below.

Feedback form

10A Q&A sessions

9 Evaluate your own and others' handling of questions from the audience using the feedback form below.

Feedback form

10B Q&A sessions

9 Evaluate your own and others' handling of questions from the audience using the feedback form below.

Acknowledgements

Author's acknowledgements

Where do I begin? My special thanks go to the commissioning editor Chris Capper for his championing of this title and unwavering support throughout; to the project manager Will Capel for his editorial wisdom and heartening belief in the material; to my editor Alison Silver with her eagle eye for detail and tireless efficiency; to the production controller Julie Sontag for steering the project to completion; to the proofreader Marcus Fletcher for a thorough and professional job; and to the permissions clearance controller Chris Doggett, who literally made it his mission to track down every last expert I wanted to feature in the course and secure their approval. For a fresh and vibrant book design I have senior designer Claire Parson and picture researcher Hilary Luckcock to thank, as well as John Park, the studio manager at eMC Design Ltd. And for skilfully producing the accompanying audio recordings my thanks go to Leon Chambers and The Soundhouse Studios. I'd also like to thank Simon Kent of London Metropolitan University for first putting me on to Quentin Willson's superlative summary of the E-Type Jaguar and Carl Dowse of the Fachhochschule für Ökonomie und Management in Essen for introducing me to more presentation websites and YouTube clips than I can mention. I must, of course, extend my gratitude to the many presentation experts who agreed to be quoted, in some cases extensively, in this book. These people are true leaders in the field of public speaking and I am delighted to have them appear on these pages. After all that, I've saved up the last bit of thanks for my wife, Begoña – always there for me, an audience of one, but still the best audience I've ever faced.

Publisher's acknowledgements

The author and publishers acknowledge the following sources of copyright material and are grateful for the permissions granted. While every effort has been made, it has not always been possible to identify the sources of all the material used, or to trace all copyright holders. If any omissions are brought to our notice, we will be happy to include the appropriate acknowledgements on reprinting.

Andrew Leigh for the text on p6, reproduced with permission of Andrew Leigh, www.maynardleigh.co.uk; Sonya Hamlin for the adapted text on p8 from *How to Talk so People Listen: Connecting in Today's Workplace* by Sonya Hamlin; Andy Bounds, communication expert, for the text on p9, reproduced with permission; Quentin Willson for the text on p9, reproduced with permission; Rob Geraghty for the text on p10, reproduced with permission; Gerry Spence for the text on p14, reproduced with permission; Doug Jefferys for the text on p14, reproduced with permission, www.PublicSpeakingSkills.com; Louise Mahler for the text on p15, reproduced with permission; Timothy Koegel for the text on p16, reproduced with permission; text on p17 from *Other People's Money* by Jerry Sterner, copyright © 1989 Jerry Sterner; T.J. Walker for the text on p18, reproduced with permission; Nancy Duarte for the text on pp19 and 24, reproduced with permission; Don McMillan for the text on p20, reproduced with permission; Seth Godin for the text on p20, reproduced with permission; Tom Peters for the text on p22, reproduced with permission; Garr Reynolds for the text on p22, reproduced with permission; Carmine Gallo for the text on p23, reproduced with permission; Begoña Arsuaga for the text on p26, reproduced with permission; Carol Kinsey Goman, PhD, author of *The Nonverbal Advantage: Secrets and Science of Body Language at Work*, for the text on p26; Joe Navarro, former FBI Special agent and author *of What Every BODY is Saying* and *Louder Than Words* for the text on p28; Dr Nick Morgan for the text on p30, reproduced with permission; Mike Grabiner for the text on p30, reproduced with permission; Doni Tamblyn for the text on p32, reproduced with permission; Tracy Goodwin for the text on p34, reproduced with permission; text on p34 taken from *Dr No* by Ian Fleming © Ian Fleming Publications Ltd 1958, reprinted with permission from Ian Fleming Publications Ltd; Max Atkinson for the text on p36, reproduced with permission; the Estate of Roberto Goizueta and Coca-Cola for the text on p37, reproduced with permission; Patsy Rodenburg for the text on p40, reproduced with permission; Richard Holmes and Stefan Schwartz for the text from *Shooting Fish* on p40; Text on p40 from *Wall Street* ©1987 Courtesy of Twentieth Century Fox. Written by Stanley Weiser & Oliver Stone. All rights reserved. Excerpt from 'Thank You for Smoking' ©2005 Courtesy of Twentieth Century Fox. Written by Jason Reitman. All rights reserved; Room 9 Entertainment for *Thank You for Smoking*; Carly Fiorina for the text on p41, reproduced

with permission; Dr Howard Gardner for the text on p42, reproduced with permission; Stephen Denning for the text on p42, reproduced with permission; Ed Brodow for the text on p43, Ed Brodow is a negotiation expert, keynote speaker, and bestselling author of *Negotiation Boot Camp*. Copyright © 2010 Ed Brodow. All rights reserved; Annette Simmons for the text on p44, reproduced with permission; Jerry Weissman for the text on p46, reproduced with permission; Kees Garman for the text on p46, reproduced with permission; Sue Gaulke, President, Successworks for the text on p48. Excerpt from *101 Ways to Captivate a Business Audience* copyright, Successworks www.successworksusa.com; Majorie Scardino for the text on p48 from *That Presentation Sensation* by Martin Conradi and Richard Hall; Tom Antion for the text on p49, reproduced with permission; Sir Ken Robinson for the text on p90, reproduced with permission; Nigel Barlow for the text on p91, reproduced with permission.

The publishers are grateful to the following for permission to reproduce copyright photographs and material:

Key: l = left, r = right, t = top, c = centre, b = bottom

Alamy/©PhotoAlto for p4(br), /©Fancy for p4(cl), /©BlueMoon Stock for p9(b), /©The Art Gallery Collection for p14(tl), /©Photoplusminus for p18(b), /©Images Bazaar for p19(t), /©Inspirestock Inc for p21, /©Andia for p26(b), /©Rubberball for p27(all), /©Cultura for p29(t)(b), /©Bob Pardue-Lifestyle for p29(t)(c), /©Inmagine for p29(t)(f), /©moodboard for p29(t)(g), /©Blend Images for p29(t)(j), /©Glowimages for p29(t)(l), /©Tetra Images for p29(t)(n), /©Mike stone for p29(t)(h), /©First Light for p29(b)(c), /©eStock Photo for p29(b)(d), /©PhotoAlto for p33, /©Radius Images for p39(1), /©Blend Images for p39(4), /©Image Source for p66, /©Mohamad Itani for p83(tr), /©Ace Stock Ltd for p85, /©UpperCut Images for p86(t), /©moodboard for p86(c), /©Jim Wileman for p86(b); Corbis/©Bettmann for p14(tr), /©Kimberly White for p19(b), /©Bettmann for p20(b), /©Sunset Boulevard for p34(b), /©Melanie Burford/Dallas Morning News for p35, /©Louie Psihoyos for p37, /©The Art Archive for p38(t), /©Kim Kulish for p38(b), /©Chris Farina for p41, /©Lew Robertson for p83(br), /©Frederic Cirou/PhotoAlto, /©Tom Grill for p42(b), /©Frederic Cirou/PhotoAlto for p89; Getty Images for p40(ct); Getty Images/©Time and Life Pictures for p6(r), /©Ron Chapple for p18(c), /©Peter Dazeley for p39(3), /©Bill Curtsinger for p83(cr); istockphoto/©Pano Karapanagiotis for p12, /©Jeremy Edwards for p19(ct), /©Gino Santa Maria for p29(t)(a), /©Color and CopySpace for p29(t)(i), /©Silvia Boratti for p29(t)(k), /©Jan Will for p29(b)(a); Kobal Collection/©Warner Bros for p17(l & r), /©20th Century Fox for p40(cb); Philips for p78(l); Philips Lumalive for p79(tl); Photolibrary/©Image DJ for p29(t)(m), /©Kristian Pohl for p29(b)(e); Punchstock/©Bananastock for p32(b); Rex Features for p9(c); Rex Features/©Erik Pendzich for p11(t), /©Peter Brooker for p40(t); Ronald Grant Archive/©Room 9 Entertainment for p40(b); Shutterstock/©Monkey Business Images for p11(b), /©StockLite for p22(b), /©Rui Vale de Sousa for p29(t)(d), /©Steve Cukrow for p29(t)(e), /©Ralf Juergen Kraft for p29(b)(b), /©Andresr for p39(2), /©Stephen Coburn for p39(5), /©Felix Mizioznikov for p62, /©StockLite for p67, /©Supri Suharjoto for p78(r), /©Ljupco Smokovski for p79(tr).

We have been unable to trace the copyright holder for the photos on p88 and would welcome any information enabling us to do so.

Picture research by Hilary Luckcock.

The publisher has used its best endeavours to ensure that the URLs for external websites referred to in this book are correct and active at the time of going to press. However, the publisher has no responsibility for the websites and can make no guarantee that a site will remain live or that the content is or will remain appropriate.